# WH[illegible] CARES?



To Tony Thanks
for your help and Support
best wishes love
Fred xx

# WHO CARES?

*Memories of a Childhood in Barnardo's*

FRED FEVER

A *Warner* Book

First published in Great Britain in 1994 by Warner Books



A CIP catalogue record for this book is available from the British Library.

ISBN 0 7515 0879 9

Typeset by M Rules
Printed and bound in Great Britain by
Clays Ltd, St Ives plc

Warner Books
A Division of
Little, Brown and Company (UK) Limited
Brettenham House
Lancaster Place
London WC2E 7EN

*This book is dedicated to adults who suffered abuse as children; to children who are currently suffering abuse; and also, unfortunately, to those children who will undoubtedly suffer abuse in the future.*

# Contents

## PART IV

# Foreword

## by Tory Laughland

When Fred Fever first telephoned me out of the blue, asking somewhat hesitantly whether he could do some voluntary work for *Who Cares?* magazine, I have to admit I was doubtful. At that time, in 1991, we had one small cramped room and far too much work to take on a person who might be unskilled. However, luckily for me, I agreed to see Fred. I realised only a short way into our conversation that he was going to be a very valuable addition to our team and I gratefully accepted his kind offer. We have had a very happy partnership ever since.

My own background as a social worker led me to start *Who Cares?* magazine in 1983 as a means of reaching young people in the care system. Through its pages, they could voice their sorrows, joys and anxieties. They could also find relevant information about their own situations and see how other young people dealt with problems. The magazine has flourished and over 20,000 copies are now bought quarterly by most of the UK social work departments for onward distribution to their young people.

From it has sprung the *Who Cares?* Trust, an independent charity dedicated to improving the cruel system about which you will read in Fred's autobiography. Again, when Fred showed the draft to me, I wondered whether I could find time to read it. Yet once I started, I could not put it down. The catalogue of unkindness, thoughtlessness and incompetence demonstrated by Fred's so-called carers (with one or two noble exceptions) holds the reader in a kind of fascinated horror from beginning to end. You wonder how anyone could survive so much change and suffering.

Yet the good news is that Fred has risen magnificently above such difficult beginnings. Starting humbly at the *Who Cares?* office with photocopying and stuffing envelopes, Fred soon graduated to giving talks to social work professionals and journalists about his care experiences. He has made a number of appearances on television, radio and in print, and he has helped to plan conferences, publications and research studies. Fred has a seat on and often chairs our Editorial Committee. He joined the Social Services Inspectorate as a 'user' inspector, and his inside knowledge is put to good use during inspections and various highly sensitive assignments.

Fred has a gift for words. He knows how to encapsulate a whole complex range of concepts and emotions into a single phrase. I'll give you an example. Speaking at the news launch for our charity, Fred was asked about the difficulties of finding housing after being in care: did he think it was easier to avoid homelessness after being in a children's home or foster family?

'Life in care is one long process of homelessness,' replied Fred, 'because you never live in your *own* home, do you?' The audience stayed silent while we thought about the pain and loneliness this answer conveyed.

Fred has gained a place at university, despite all his early miseries at school, so well documented in this book. At last things are going his way. Perhaps he is a stronger person because of all he has been through.

The care system has changed a great deal for the better since the time when Fred was going through it. But is has not changed enough: too many children and young people today still face callousness, lack of encouragement and injustice.

This book will bring a lump to your throat often; yet there is never a whiff of self-pity. This is its great strength. Not only is it an illuminating experience to read the book, but I think it will help to change the care system for the better, too.

# Acknowledgements

I wish to express my gratitude for the help, support and encouragement of the following people, who helped make this book possible: Susan Gilchrist, Nigel O'Mara, Dorothy Fever, Jean Wylie, Elizabeth Wylie, Neil Gatenby, Beryl Spence, Polly Steele, Ben Hall, Tory Laughland, John Simms, Octavia Wiseman, Sandy Violette, Alan Samson and Caroline North.

# Introduction

In June [illegible] [illegible] [illegible] [illegible]

[illegible]

[illegible] [illegible] explode [illegible] the [illegible]

# Introduction

In July 1987, child sexual abuse in Cleveland hit the national headlines. The mass media focused much attention on the subject from then on and I was surprised by the vast amount of media coverage it received. My second surprise was how the general public began openly discussing the sexual abuse of children; after having been a taboo subject it became and still is very topical.

The sudden interest stimulated parts of my mind that I had closed. At the time I was working for a large company in their reprographic department. Due to the lack of mental stimulation offered by photocopying I began to think back to my own past as a child. I recalled the greater part of my life, which was spent in the care of Dr Barnardo's. Throughout the years I lived in care I had been treated very well by some people and abused by others. Getting away from the thoughts, memories and feelings about abuse became almost impossible: it was on television, in the newspapers, on the radio, people were talking about it everywhere; it was on my mind day and night.

By the summer of 1988 I was on the verge of a nervous breakdown. I could no longer function normally. I was about to explode – the emotional turmoil inside my head had to be released somehow. Insomnia replaced sleep and I was losing weight at a quite alarming rate. I was very ill and desperately needed help, and eventually I admitted this to myself. I could no longer ignore the signs that were self-evident. My supervisor at work noticed the changes in me and we discussed the situation. She suggested that I talked to someone at Barnardo's. I didn't want to – after all I saw them as the root cause of my problems, for it was in their care that the abuse happened. After giving the idea a great deal of thought I decided I would go and see a person I knew at Barnardo's head office. I still had my reservations, but out of sheer desperation and the absence of any alternatives I summoned all my courage and contacted them.

On 8 July 1988 I made my way to Barnardo's head office in Barkingside. Somehow I managed to get lost en route and arrived very late for my appointment. The woman I had arranged to meet holds a high position within Barnardo's. Because of my late arrival and her busy work schedule, we were able to have only a short discussion. The outcome of our meeting was that I would go over to Barkingside again and talk to the Barnardo's senior social worker counsellor about my past. On my second visit introductions were made and I began to talk to a counsellor. From the outset it was quite clear that I would need some ongoing counselling. We arranged to meet again a couple of weeks later. My counsellor thought it would be of benefit to me and to her if she read through my entire file and wrote a brief background history of my life in care. By 2 August the task was completed, so we met again and I read through what my counsellor had written. We discussed my file and what was in it and what had clearly been left out.

I read what was supposed to be my background history, taken from my file, many times, and decided that there was something wrong. Vast chunks of my experiences in care had gone unwritten; blatant lies were in my file. At this point I was feeling angry, frustrated and resentful towards Barnardo's. The counselling wasn't going very well and I was again feeling at odds with the organisation. I felt I could not just sit there and do nothing. It was during this time that I decided to write the full, true account of my life in the care of Dr Barnardo's. I first put pen to paper on 24 August 1988, but didn't start in earnest until early November 1988.

I began to write my autobiography as a form of self-counselling. As time went on I realised that what I was writing might help others who had been through similar experiences. I then decided to break the silence, the silence expected of abuse victims.

The aim of this book is to contribute to the growing knowledge of child abuse. It is an account of my first sixteen years of life, and it details my experiences of child abuse in the care of Dr Barnardo's.

The facts are laid out before you as I experienced them at the time. In writing them down, I have been trying to find the answers to two questions: Why? And how? Why did such things go on, and why and how were they allowed to happen in places where children are put for their own safety and protection?

# Author's Note

My book begins with a short story about my mother and father, even though I didn't find out most of what I have written about my parents until I was in my mid-twenties. The reason I begin here is that had my parents been different, my life would have taken a completely different course. I was given very little information while growing up in care, but later discovered the details when researching this book. My father's sister, Dorothy Fever, was most helpful in providing me with background knowledge of my parents. My official files from Barnardo's also provided some useful information which helped me piece together the reasons why the organisation became my legal guardian.

It is important to note that the majority of children are taken into care because their parents are unable to look after them properly, not because the child has done anything wrong to warrant being placed into care.

The names in this book have been changed, with the exception of those of myself and my family members. This has been done for reasons which will become clear later.

---

*A note regarding the illustrations:*
The only photos I have of my childhood in care are of me when I was a baby until the age of seven. Thereafter no photos were taken of me; nobody seemed to think it worthwhile.

# PART I

# 1

# In the Beginning

My father, Albert William Fever, worked for the council doing various labouring jobs such as road-sweeping, refuse-collecting and gardening. He had had very little formal education and was totally illiterate. However, he worked hard at his jobs. Apparently he had a quick temper and would fly into a rage when things went wrong, but afterwards was always quick to apologise.

During the summer of 1963, at the age of forty-four, my father went into hospital for a minor operation. It was there that he met my mother, Freda. Freda Lizzie Paine was thirty-six, but her physical appearance suggested that she was much older, perhaps in her mid-fifties. In stark contrast to her appearance she had the mental age of a child. Freda was introduced to Albert by her father, who occupied the hospital bed next to his. Their courtship took place during the regular visits Freda made to see her father, who seemed more than pleased to see his daughter embarking on a new romance. The bizarre nature of their short courtship had little effect on their intentions. Within a week of leaving hospital, Albert Fever was making arrangements to marry Freda Paine.

My mother had been married before, to a Mr Paine, by whom she gave birth to two sons. The first child did not live very long, not even long enough to see his first birthday. This was because she used to take the child to bed with her, although she had been told not to. On one fatal night she took the child to bed with her for the last time. In the morning her baby was dead. My mother had accidentally suffocated her first child.

Later on in the marriage my mother gave birth to her second child, who also never saw his first birthday. At the age of three months he died of malnutrition and pneumonia. Throughout his short life he was probably rarely, if ever, fed properly, and can never have known comfort or contentment. My mother and her first husband later separated.

When my parents' wedding day arrived, neither my grandmother nor my father's sister, Dorothy, had met Freda. Albert's mother wasn't keen for this wedding to go ahead, but found herself anyway at the register office. It was not a lavish wedding – nobody had any flowers, not even a buttonhole.

When it was time for the witnesses to sign the book, Albert's mother refused on the grounds that she didn't want her son to marry this woman. Albert's sister Dorothy took her aside and explained that if she didn't sign, all they needed to do was fetch a stranger off the street and that would be good enough. In the end my Aunt Dorothy, reluctantly, and Freda's father signed the book. There was no proper reception, just tea and sandwiches at Freda's father's house. Albert and Freda were now Mr and Mrs Fever.

My parents had no home of their own, so after the wedding they lived with my mother's father, Mr Caplin. Mr Caplin was difficult to live with. He was bad-tempered and tyrannical and controlled the lives of my parents in every respect, and even took money from them which was not rightly his. All this did nothing to help an already difficult marital situation between my parents, who had frequent arguments.

In later years, when my parents lived in their own house, it was not uncommon for my mother to lock my father out. He would have to sleep in the shed, then go to work the next day without so much as a wash. The people at work found out why my father was unshaven and would try to help him.

My parents were still living at Mr Caplin's house when I was born on 16 June 1964. They were out walking nearby when my mother went into premature labour. They managed to get home and soon afterwards I was born, weighing only 4lb 3oz. My mother and I were rushed to Farnborough Hospital, where I was placed in the incubator in which I was to remain for over three months until I put on weight and was well enough to leave hospital.

I was regularly visited by my father and my Aunt Dorothy, and my grandmother also came. The last time she ever saw me I was in an incubator and my Aunt Dorothy did not meet me again for many years.

On seeing my mother, the hospital head social worker decided to look into her case, and it soon became apparent that she was not capable of looking after a baby, especially a sick baby. The social worker was also aware of my mother's record of looking after babies. A meeting was arranged to discuss the case of Alfred James Fever. At this meeting people from the medical profession decided that because of her history, my mother was clearly incapable of caring for me and could not be allowed to take me home.

The head social worker then contacted the local authority to try to place me into their care. But the local authority would not accept me because there had been no damage done to me by my parents. The fact that it was very likely that something *would* happen was not their concern; they would take action only after such an event.

The social worker was unhappy with the local authority's unhelpful attitude and Dr Barnardo's were approached. My case was discussed and it was decided that I should be taken into care until I was a bit stronger, when I would be allowed to go home to my parents. The agreement by which I was put into care was a 'voluntary agreement', which meant that both parties concerned agreed that this should happen. On 25 September 1964, I left Farnborough Maternity Department and was discharged into the care of Dr Barnardo's. I had not spent even one day at home with my parents. Dr Barnardo's placed me in St Christopher's nursery in Tunbridge Wells, and my life in care began.

*

My early years with Dr Barnardo's were happy and secure. St Christopher's children's home offered a new approach to child care back in the 1960s. It was completely different from the big old institutions which had lots of children in one large house, and were run like something out of a Dickens novel. St Christopher's consisted of many small houses, each of which had two house parents who looked after seven or eight children. As well as the house parents there were daily helpers. The main idea of having house parents was to try to create an environment which was closer to a normal family home.

Most of the houses were newly built when I was admitted to St Christopher's. The nursery, where I lived for the first part of my life, was part of a large building which dominated the main drive. It also housed the head office, and the basement which was used as a food store. As well as the individual houses and the nursery, the complex contained a nursery school, playing fields, tennis courts, woods, a large hall and a car park with garages.

At the age of about twelve months I was moved to Domaris, a brand-new house within the complex. The house was large in comparison with an average three-bedroomed semi. The downstairs floor was divided into two parts: the main area was for the children, while the other part, where the house parents lived, was off-limits unless you had permission to go there. It was just like a normal home, apart from the separate accommodation for the house parents. The spacious living-room/playroom had large seats which were used as toy cupboards. The dining-room led in from the playroom in an L shape. There was a hatch from the kitchen into the dining-room for food to be passed through. The kitchen was very large. The back door led into the kitchen and the children always went in and out using that entrance. Downstairs there was also a cloakroom and toilet. In the cloakroom we had pegs to hang our coats on and space for our boots and shoes. The stairs to the bedrooms were in a large hallway where the front door and telephone were. Upstairs there were five bedrooms, one bathroom, a toilet and a large landing with cupboards. One of the bedrooms slept three children, one took two and the other three bedrooms slept one child in each. Domaris had a large front garden, surrounded by a four-foot high white fence, with a shed and a small sand-pit. The large back garden was on a hill.

The house parents in Domaris up to 1971 were Jenny and Peter Cole. Jenny had herself been in Dr Barnardo's as a child. She had helped to look after me and other babies in the nursery, and when Domaris was ready Jenny took me and some of the other children there and set about making a home for us all. I don't know how old Jenny was then but she probably would have been in her early twenties. She had a warm, friendly face and a lovely smile. She always had, or made, time for us children; she gave me love and was a very wonderful mother to me. She had many outstanding qualities: she was generous, fair, approachable and very caring, and she also had a wonderful sense of humour. She had lots of patience, and if we got a telling-off from Jenny you can bet we well deserved it. On the whole, life at Domaris with Jenny was a very happy one indeed.

Jenny's husband, Peter, the son of a farmer, was in the building trade. He now has his own business. Peter was a giant of a man; his size seemed overwhelming when I was a young child, but he was very gentle and I have no recollection of him ever hitting any of us. He was a very kind and generous man. Jenny and Peter were not married when she first worked at St Christopher's, and when he first moved into Domaris, I'm told I was quite put out. But I soon became accustomed to this new person in 'my' house. As the house mother Jenny was there all the time, while Peter went out to work and we only saw him in the evenings and at weekends. In that respect I suppose my early life was not unlike that of a child in a conventional family, albeit with a lot of brothers and sisters. I was always aware that Jenny was not my 'real' mother, but I certainly loved her as any child loves its mother.

One of the earliest memories I have of Domaris is potty training. I can remember it very clearly, although I was less than two years old. The other children and I would have to sit on our potties until there was some evidence that we had done something. I think all the potties were the same colour, yellow. Our potties were put on the floor in the cloakroom, which happened to be next to the toilet. I think there was some psychological reasoning behind this, the idea being that the children could see where they would progress to once they got the hang of going on the potty.

If you had been sitting on your potty for a long while without anything to show for it you were given encouragement to do some 'big jobs'. The encouragement came in the form of a promised sweet, which was given to you when you offered proof of your labours. The only trouble with this was that if you got up off your potty to wander about and without realising it had left a 'big job' behind, someone might take your potty and claim your sweet. Nicking each other's potties happened quite often, so towards the end of potty training the use of sweets as an incentive was stopped.

In 1968 I left St Christopher's for a short period to be fostered by a family. The one memory I have of this time is being wheeled around in a wheelbarrow by my foster father. For some reason which I never knew about the foster home broke down after only a short time and I was put back into care. Once back at Domaris I soon settled down.

I have fond memories of nursery school. I enjoyed painting and loved the bright colours. Being very shy, I preferred my own company at school. Outside the nursery school there was a playground, sand-pit and a large cage with two little guinea pigs in it. I did not like the playground as the children were a bit rough, and the sand-pit I disliked because the sand got everywhere it was not supposed to go. But I loved the guinea pigs; they were just excellent. I would sit by their cage whenever I could, listening to them making squeaky noises. Now and again the teacher would get them out and the other children and I were allowed to stroke them. As far as I was concerned, this was one of the highlights of nursery school. The house parents took great care of the small ones: I was always taken to and collected from school by someone, even though the nursery school was within the St Christopher's complex. One day someone upset me and I ran away. When I got home Jenny told me off – not because I had missed school but for coming home on my own.

As a young child I often listened to the radio, and would dance and sing along to the music. The first song I remember hearing was 'Where's Your Mama Gone'. The song went something like this:

> Where's your mama gone, where's your mama gone?
> Far far away.
>
> Last night I heard my mama singing this song
> Oo-wee chirpy chirpy cheep cheep
>
> Woke up in the morning and my mama was gone
> Oo-wee chirpy chirpy cheep cheep
> Chirpy chirpy cheep cheep now
>
> Where's your mama gone, where's your mama gone?
> Far far away.

At the time the words didn't mean anything to me, but on reflection I think it is quite poignant that this particular song has always stuck in my mind.

# 2

# Early Antics

The other children who lived in Domaris with me up to 1971 were John, Clare, Julie, Steven and David. There was also another girl, but I cannot remember her name or anything about her.

John was a year older than me. As a youngster he was very mischievous, always up to something. Being of a similar age, we became very close friends and would go around together quite a lot. In many ways, during the early part of my life at St Christopher's, John was like an older brother to me. We knew we were not real brothers but we had a fraternal relationship which was quite strong.

Clare was a really sweet little girl. We were not like brother and sister – our relationship was more like that of a boyfriend and girlfriend. In those early years she was the loveliest girl I knew. She was extremely pretty and the memory that is most prominent in my mind is her beautiful smile. Like me, Clare was one of the babies Jenny had brought from the nursery to live in Domaris, and so she and I were brought up together.

Julie had the same colour hair and eyes as me. She was severely deaf; she wore a hearing aid and because of her disability her speech was fairly limited. I got on very well with Julie; we were like brother and sister. In times of difficulty she and I would stick up for one another.

Steven stayed at Domaris only at weekends and during school holidays. The rest of the time he was at boarding school. We hardly saw each other so I have few memories of him. David was about seven years older than me. He looked absolutely massive and stood six feet tall, maybe taller. Because of the age gap I did not have much contact with him during my early years at Domaris.

In all children's homes there is a certain amount of movement and fluctuation in numbers. Often children go back to live with their parents, or are fostered out, or are moved to a different children's home. Not all of the children I've described lived at Domaris all the time I was there. As well as the other children and house parents there were other members of staff who helped to run the house and look after the children, yet I have no clear memories of particular staff members during my early years.

Although my full name is Alfred James Fever, I was never called Alfred, always Fred. I have not been known as Alfred since I was very little. Once when I was on my way into town with a member of staff an old lady stopped us for a chat. She said, 'Oh, that's a nice little boy. What's his name?'

'Alfred James Fever,' the staff member replied.

Then the stranger went on to tell me about Alfred the Great and how he burnt the cakes. I would not have minded, but I had heard this story many times before and was getting tired of it. This is the last time I have any recollection of being called Alfred, except by official bodies.

As a youngster I often went to the local park, as did many of the children from St Christopher's. The park was just across the road, and to a small child it seemed really huge. I was too young to go to the park alone, so I was always accompanied by a staff member or Jenny. There was a large lake with boats and ducks on it. I often fed the ducks and it was a rare treat to go out in a boat.

In the less frequented part of Dullaland Park there is a monument. It is a pure white statue of a woman who drowned in the lake, at least that is what I was told. The statue was encased in a structure made mostly of glass. I was fascinated by this statue and always wanted to go and see it whenever I visited the park. From the first time I saw it I wanted to get inside the glass and touch the statue. I don't know why it captivated me so much – perhaps it was because the woman looked so peaceful. I loved Dullaland Park and never tired of going there, or of looking at the statue.

The children at St Christopher's were sometimes taken out on day trips, and once we went on an outing to London. Peter drove Jenny, John, Clare and me, as I remember, up to London in his car. As we drew nearer to the city, the traffic increased, and the noise, and the number of people streaming across the streets. It was scary, but also exhilarating. I was beside myself with excitement when I saw a man standing way, way above the teeming streets, gazing into the distance.

'What's that man doing on top of that pole?' I shouted.

Jenny replied, 'That's Nelson's Column.'

'Yes,' I insisted, 'but what is he doing up there?'

Jenny explained that as he was a statue he was not doing anything. Everyone had a good laugh about the man up the pole. This episode was often referred to, and became a source of much amusement at Domaris.

In the evening we went to a restaurant, which was a rare treat. We all had a great day and I learnt a thing or two!

Jenny and Peter married in the early part of 1968. I was only three when the wedding took place. Beforehand there was a big build-up, and John had a key role to play: he was going to be the page boy. The page boy had specific tasks to perform and also had special clothes to wear. I didn't understand why there could be only one page boy. I approached Jenny on the matter. I felt pretty envious of John when I saw his page boy outfit and I asked Jenny if I could be a page boy too. Jenny went to great lengths to explain weddings to me and why there could be only one page boy. I asked why John had been chosen and not me. Jenny said that I was too young. I was upset, but by the time the wedding took place, I had come to accept that it wasn't possible for me to be a page boy. I have very little memory of the wedding day itself. All I remember is us standing outside the church having our photographs taken.

In 1969 someone bought identical summer outfits for John

and me. They were blue T-shirts with thin white stripes, blue cotton shorts and blue canvas shoes. I am not sure who it was who gave the outfit its name, or why, but it was known as the Buster Bill suit. John and I enjoyed wearing our Buster Bill suits, probably because we liked the name and also because we associated them with going out somewhere special. We couldn't wear what we liked: a member of staff or Jenny would set out our clothes every night, so when we got up in the morning what we would wear that day had already been decided. The Buster Bill suits were worn only on outings and day trips. So whenever John and I went to bed and saw them laid out for the morning we would go off to sleep quite excited at the prospect of a treat the next day.

One perfect day remains in my memory. The previous evening Peter had made me a ship out of scrap wood. In the morning John and I put on our Buster Bill suits and that afternoon we went out and I took my ship and sailed it on a small pond. That day is a distillation, I suppose, of the happiness and security of my early childhood.

As well as Jenny and Peter another adult played her part in giving me some happy memories in my first few years at St Christopher's. Pauline Baker was training to be a nurse. For a time she lived at St Christopher's, which in those days had accommodation for student nurses. I had a very close friendship with her: she was like a mother to me, although not to the same extent as Jenny Cole, for she could not devote as much time to me as could Jenny, who was always there. Given the chance I think Pauline would have spent more time with me than she already did. She was caring, warm, friendly, loving and kind. I trusted her and knew that she always had my best interests at heart.

Pauline often took me out to places around Tunbridge Wells. After we got to know each other she took me home to her parents' house in Gravesend for weekends. I remember going down to the river nearby. It always looked beautiful down by the river. I felt very much at peace there on those warm summer evenings. Once Pauline took me to the pictures, to see *The*

*Tales of Beatrix Potter*, and I was enthralled by the film and its wonderful characters. When I stayed at Pauline's house during the holidays she would put me to bed and then read me a story from *Winnie the Pooh* or *The House at Pooh Corner*. One Christmas I stayed at Pauline's house, and that was probably one of the best Christmases I have ever experienced.

On Christmas Day Pauline and her family and I went to the local church a couple of minutes' walk from the house. Then it was Christmas dinner, and Christmas pudding and presents, and as the visiting child I was the centre of attention, which was rare. It even snowed that year, too, and on Boxing Day we built a snowman. It was fun to make and looked quite splendid when we had finished it.

Although I wasn't very old when I knew Pauline, I can remember how special a person she was to me. I still think about her with much love and affection. She was a very important figure in my childhood and I feel eternally grateful to her for those memorable times we spent together.

St Christopher's, being a Dr Barnardo's home, had strongly held religious attitudes. Every Sunday, all the children had to go to church with no exceptions; unless, of course, you were ill. You wore specific clothes to church – your 'Sunday best' – and you weren't allowed to wear them on any other days. I do not remember much about church in this early stage of my life, except it all seemed strange and daunting. After church we would go home for Sunday lunch, which I can recall vividly because we had stripey ice-cream. We always had an interesting flavour ice-cream on Sundays. Peter would buy it when he went to get the Sunday papers, and sometimes I was allowed to go in the car with him, which was an extra Sunday treat.

During my first few years at St Christopher's a charitable organisation held an annual Christmas party for all us kids. This included not only a Christmas present but also transport to and from the party at a place called Paddock Wood. The first one I remember I didn't really enjoy; I was a shy child, and the huge hall, which rang with the excited shrieks of what seemed like hundreds of boisterous unknown children, was strange and overwhelming. The wooden trestle tables always groaned with nice things to eat, not to mention lots of crackers. Above the tables, suspended from the ceiling, hung a huge net, which ran the full length of the hall. Inside were hundreds and hundreds of multi-coloured balloons.

When everyone had finished eating and drinking, party games would be played, and afterwards, just before it was time to go home, the balloons were released by the organisers. For me this was the best bit of the party. The balloons being let out of the net really finished it in style with a magnificent mass of uncontrollable colours.

As a young child I thought of primary school as 'big' school. Ever since John had started primary school I had looked forward to going there myself. John, being a year older than me, started a year before me, and consequently I heard all about 'big school' before I went. I felt a bit left out when I couldn't start 'big school' at the same time as John, but eventually my big day arrived. I got dressed except for my tie – Jenny tied that for me, as I had absolutely no idea of how to do it. We were ready to go off to school when Jenny decided to take a photograph of John and me. I was pleased: I was wearing my brand-new uniform and excited at the prospect of my first day at school, and I was all for having my photo taken. John, on the other hand, didn't like the idea one little bit; in fact he was quite adamant that he was not going to pose for the camera. Clearly he felt that he was far too much of an old hand to have a fuss made about such a trivial occurrence as going to school. 'It's not my first day at school so I don't see why I should have my photo taken,' he argued. Eventually, after some friendly persuasion, John gave in and we went outside. We stood in the warm sun under a familiar tree, waiting for the camera's approval. We had identical uniforms; the only difference was that mine was spanking new. As the sun shone upon us I basked in the glory of the occasion. Within a matter of seconds it was over. The camera had captured the moment, and it was time to go to school.

I have no recollection of my first day at St Peter's Primary School, although I do remember my early years there with some affection. The school had very close links with the nearby St Peter's Church. The playground and dining hall were separate from the school and we had to walk down a short road to reach them. On the way we passed a sweet shop, always thronged with children and doing a brisk trade in traffic-light lollies, blackjacks, fruit gums and sherbet dips.

The school was very old. St Peter's had a total of about six classrooms, including a large class at the top of the building with two teachers. It also had a library, and a staff room which was used for watching television. There was also a small area for pottery classes. Most of the furniture in the school had seen a good many years. Outside the main building there were steps leading down to what appeared to be dungeons but were in fact the boys' toilets, although in truth they bore a closer resemblance to dungeons than toilets.

St Peter's Church was directly opposite the school playground. It was rather grand with a very tall spire. The interior always looked immaculate. I remember vividly the annual Harvest Festival, perhaps because it was different from the usual services. All the children had to make a contribution of produce and the church looked odd festooned with food, the scent of fruit mingling with the usual musty, churchy smell.

At St Peter's Church of England Primary School a certain amount of Christianity was introduced into our daily lives. At the end of each day the teacher would say a prayer before sending us home, and before prayers all the chairs had to be stacked neatly on top of the tables. Prayers wouldn't be said until there was complete silence. Then the teacher would begin. She always started by saying, 'Hands together, eyes closed.' One day, the chairs on the tables and complete silence reigning in the classroom, the teacher gave her 'Hands together, eyes closed,' introduction, and I added, '. . . and don't forget to blow your nose!' in a loud voice.

The teacher shouted: 'Fred! You had better stay behind when all the others have gone.' When the other children in the class had stopped laughing and were quiet again she said the prayer, and afterwards all the children left the classroom except me. I was told that I had been very naughty and that my punishment for disrupting the class was to take all the chairs off the tables and put them back on again, without making a noise. I also had to say sorry before being allowed to go home. I quickly carried out my punishment and then apologised to the teacher. I didn't mind the punishment, but I wanted to get out of the classroom so that I could laugh about it with my friends.

One lunchtime, in the dinner hall, John and I got into a bit of trouble. I don't remember what the first course was but I do remember the pudding, which that day consisted of a pastry with white mock cream topping. Someone confided that the white stuff on the pudding was shaving foam. Gingerly, John and I had a small taste of the white topping. John was sitting at the far end of the table and I was a few seats further down, but I was close enough to see the disgust on his face after the first spoonful. I didn't like the taste of it either. John said emphatically: 'It's shaving foam!' The next thing I knew he was liberally plastering his face with the cream.

Instinctively, I plunged my hands into my own pudding and mirrored John's actions. Then the two of us started laughing: we did look funny sitting in the dinner hall with all the other children around us, our faces plastered with sticky white topping. We started addressing comments to each other and the other children about how manly we were: men shave, we said, and we now had shaving foam on our faces. I was aged about five and John six at the time. Then suddenly both of us were pulled from our seats by two dinner ladies and marched out of the dining area. When they asked us why we had spread our pudding on our faces we told them straight: 'It's shaving cream!'

The dinner ladies replied: 'No, it's not, it's pudding.'

Our explanation was that the other children had told us it was shaving foam. We had our hands and faces forcibly washed by the dinner ladies with a large, smelly dishcloth. When both of us had been cleaned up we were told not to be silly and to act sensibly when having our lunch. We both apologised and said we wouldn't do it again.

Another break time I had a loose tooth in the school playground. I was on my own and nobody was bothering me so I decided now would be a good time to sort out that annoying wiggly tooth, which had been irritating me for a number of days. I sat in the sun, vigorously wiggling the tooth with my thumb and forefinger. These moments of quiet reflection were not to last however, and John arrived on the scene. He asked what I was doing. When I told him I was trying to wiggle my tooth out he suggested that I let him punch it out – it would be easy, he said. I didn't go much on John's idea. It sounded painful. He egged me on. 'Go on, it won't hurt you, I'll punch it out, show me which one it is.' I didn't enlighten him – frankly I didn't want that sort of tooth extraction.

'If I knock it out you can put it under your pillow and you'll get half a crown, but we could share the money as I helped knock it out,' he explained. Now I realised why he was so keen to help me. I told him that I didn't want his help and that I would carry on wiggling it. The tooth eventually came out, but through my wiggling and the course of time there was no pain involved, and I got all the proceeds myself.

On another occasion I was passing the time of day quietly in the playground when suddenly – crash! bang! wallop! – I was sent flying across the playground by a rather large boy who was playing football. He had gone for the ball but had collided with me. I ended up in a heap on the ground, my head hitting the corner of a wooden shed with some force. Within seconds I was on my feet. The boy asked if I was OK and I said I was. I didn't think any more of it until John ran up to me. 'You've got blood on your shirt!' he exclaimed.

'Where? Where is the blood?'

'On your collar round the back.'

I gingerly put my hand around the back of my head to feel the damp, warm wetness that was seeping from the wound. I brought my hand in front of my face and saw the blood trickling over my fingers. My hair was sticky and matted: there was no doubt about it, there was blood oozing from my head.

John took me to the monitors, the dinner ladies or teachers who supervised the playground. It was decided that I needed medical treatment. Within minutes it had all been arranged, and a teacher drove me to hospital. I was seen in the casualty department by a very kind nurse who cleaned and stitched the wound. I was a little frightened but the nurse put me at ease. Being in hospital was quite an adventure. I didn't much like the smell of disinfectant, but the people were very nice. I had two stitches but it seemed a lot more at the time. Afterwards I had a cup of tea with the nurse. By this time Jenny had arrived to pick me up. The nurse and I had quickly become friends, and I was surprised and thrilled when she invited me to come to her house for tea when my head was better. Jenny, who was relieved to see that I was all right, took me home, and a couple of weeks later I went to the nurse's house for tea. It was a smashing afternoon and I really enjoyed myself.

St Christopher's was a paradise for kids in that there was a wonderful wood to play in bordering the complex, not to mention some magnificent trees in the grounds themselves. To us, tree-climbing wasn't just a pastime but a competitive sport. You didn't get a prize for being able to climb further up a tree than anyone else, but the glory of having climbed higher was its own reward. John and I didn't always compete – instead of watching each other struggle, we would help each other, either by pointing out where to put a hand or foot or by pulling one another up. The only sure way of becoming proficient at tree-climbing was by practising. I must have spent many hours of my early childhood halfway up a tree.

I had been going to the 'big school' for a year, and it was the summer holidays. One day John and I stole a box of crisps from the basement stores in St Christopher's. It was John's idea, and he had a plan all worked out. We were to walk in and go straight to where the boxes of crisps were kept, on the top shelf. My job was to climb up the shelves and knock down a box for John to catch before it hit the ground. We didn't want to make any noise that would draw attention to us. John's other role was as a look-out in case any of the staff were around. We went into the stores, I climbed up the shelves, excited but nervous, and with an outstretched arm I cunningly knocked a box of crisps clean off the top shelf. John, however, failed to catch the box, and down it went with an almighty crash. Before I had even begun to climb down John was running out of the stores clutching the crisps. I quickly got down and followed him with great haste. I ran as fast as my little legs would carry me. Within minutes John and I were deep in the heart of the cool, green woods. We lay under a tree, our hearts thumping, panting and breathing in the earthy forest smell. Once we had regained our breath, John opened the box and handed me a family-sized packet of ready salted crisps. Although neither of us were hungry we ate the crisps ravenously, taking turns to keep guard. Because they were illicit they tasted particularly delicious. We were modern-day Robin Hoods, stealing crisps from the Sheriff of Nottingham and running to our hide-out in the woods. I ate three or four family-sized packets of Golden Wonder crisps, and, not surprisingly, by the time the feast was finished I felt quite sick. When both of us could eat no more we left the woods and went to play near Domaris.

As soon as we approached the house a member of staff called John and me indoors. Jenny asked us what we had been doing that morning. We didn't answer. Both of us were then sent to our bedroom. Later, Jenny came up and asked if we had stolen a box of crisps from the stores. We both denied any knowledge of the crisps. But Jenny noticed the evidence around my mouth. 'You've still got crisps on your face!' she cried. I could no longer deny that we had stolen the box. The punishment for our crime was to stay in our bedroom until we were told we could come out.

One day the staff at St Christopher's organised a day trip to the seaside. One or two children from each house went. The girls and boys were of mixed ages and I was one of the younger kids. It was a dull day but warm enough to go for a paddle. I didn't know how to swim, but everyone else was running into the sea and I wasn't going to be left out. Into the waves I went. It was freezing cold. I wanted to get out straight away until I saw that nobody else was. After a while the water felt less cold. I began to play, and before I knew what had happened I was quite a distance out to sea, and everyone and everything looked a long way away. I started to panic. 'Help! Help! Help, I can't swim!' I yelled. I was waving my arms frantically in the air when this big wave came crashing down on me. Down, down, down I went. I really thought it was the end of me. Somehow I managed to make my way towards the surface of the sea. My nose and throat convulsed as I choked on the harsh salt water. Back on the beach a member of staff had seen a glimpse of a waving arm and dived into the sea to rescue the drowning person. He must have swum very fast because as I was nearing the surface he grabbed hold of me. Within seconds I was being brought back to safety. On reaching the beach I was given a warm blanket. I didn't need mouth-to-mouth resuscitation, but I felt sick because I had swallowed a fair amount of sea water. Had it not been for my rescuer I would not be here today.

When I was about six years old I had an eye test. The test seemed weird to me, but it didn't hurt and didn't take long. Jenny and I were told that there was nothing seriously wrong with my eyes, but my eyesight was less than perfect and I would need some treatment.

I was horrified when I discovered that the treatment for correcting my poor eyesight was to be an eye patch. I had been diagnosed as having what was known as a lazy eye, where one eye was doing the other's work. What was needed to make the lazy eye work was forced labour – an eye patch over my good eye to force the lazy eye into action. I just couldn't believe it. Me, wear an eye patch? No, he must be joking, surely? When the eye specialist produced the patch, I knew it was for real. He tried to console me by telling me that people would envy me, and how other children would want an eye patch so that they too could be a pirate. I wasn't taken in by this story, not for a minute. I didn't like that patch from the moment I set my two bad eyes on it. The eye specialist put the patch on me to see how it affected my vision. I thought the treatment was exceedingly stupid. I had only one eye that I could see out of with any clarity and the eye specialist was putting a patch on it, leaving me to fumble about using my poor inadequate eye. I didn't have to wear it all the time, but that was of little consolation to me. I had to go back in six months to see if my eyesight had improved. Over the six months I wore the eye patch as little as possible. When I was given it to wear I would put it on, but as soon as no one was looking I took it off again. The other kids laughed at me; it looked ridiculous and besides, I couldn't see anything with it on.

When the six months were up Jenny and I went back to the specialist. It was decided that the eye patch would be of no further use and that I was to have a pair of glasses. I was overjoyed at the thought of getting rid of the patch and I didn't give glasses any thought at all. Having to wear glasses was a big improvement on an eye patch.

Poor eyesight was not the only medical condition that plagued me as a youngster. I also suffered from slightly spastic legs. It is possible that I inherited this abnormality. It caused me some trouble when I was young but became less of a problem as I grew older. It was once thought that I had cerebral palsy, but this theory was later dismissed. One thing is certain: there is definitely something not quite right with my legs but how severe the spasticity was I do not know.

Thrown in for good measure I also had terribly flat feet as a child. The remedy for this and my spasticity came in the form of special shoes. The shoes, as I remember, had built-up inner soles to help form an arch in my feet; but what they did for my spasticity I am not sure. They were heavy, cumbersome and ugly and I hated wearing them. Every six months I had to go to the hospital for orthopaedic treatment. I cannot remember much about it, except being told to do exercises in a gym. In between visits to the hospital I was expected to do some exercises at home, walking around the house on tiptoes for ten minutes each day. This was all supposed to correct my flat feet.

I certainly didn't like tiptoeing around the house every day looking stupid, but on the other hand I thought that it would all be worthwhile if it made a difference to my feet. And because I did the exercises they improved. The older I grew the less affected I was by the spasticity and my life was made a lot easier when I started wearing long trousers instead of shorts. The abnormality had not gone away but at least nobody could see it. From the moment I put on long trousers I never again spoke to anyone about the abnormalities in my legs.

Throughout a child's time in care, he or she is allocated a field social worker whose job it is to look after the overall welfare of that child. My first experience of field social workers was being introduced to one – and that was all. 'This is your social worker,' I was told. She said hello and then immediately sat down with the other staff and had a long chat. I can remember my name being mentioned but that was about it. My opinion was never asked for on these visits, so I just used to sit there and wait for the announcement that my social worker was going. Then I would say goodbye until the next encounter a few months later, when the same routine would be repeated.

# 3

# The End of My Childhood

The wood next to St Christopher's, which covered a good few acres of land, gave me and many other children an enormous amount of pleasure. It kept us amused for hours on end. As well as the innumerable trees there was also dense undergrowth consisting of brambles, stinging nettles, bamboo plants and other vegetation. As well as being a play area for us it also provided habitation for wildlife such as birds, squirrels and insects. I got great satisfaction and delight from the wood. In many ways it was another world, one where adults had no existence and children ruled supreme.

When I first ventured into the wood I couldn't believe my eyes, for it appeared to go on forever. Later I realised that there was a boundary, and that it wasn't infinite.

The games we played would vary according to what mood we were in. A lot of the time we didn't play games, we just went down to the wood to mess around. One day when John and I were playing in the wood I got badly stung by nettles. John showed me how to lessen the effect of the stings by spitting on a dock leaf and rubbing it on the affected area. It worked. I was impressed with John's knowledge of stinging nettles and dock leaves. He also told me that wherever stinging nettles grew somewhere nearby there would be dock leaves, and this also proved to be true.

One activity that kept us occupied in the wood was making camps. The camps were mostly built of debris and discarded wood that we found around St Christopher's. Camp-making was brilliant fun, especially when the camp was finished and we had a great new hide-out. We made our own bows and arrows from the bamboo canes that grew in the woods. When we played bows and arrows we generally played responsibly and fired the arrows at targets such as a bush or a tree but sometimes mischief prevailed and we fired them at other children. When there were enough of us with bows and arrows we played games such as Robin Hood or Jungle Warriors.

The wood was not the only place where I had fun as a youngster. There was an extensive range of rocks just a few minutes from Tunbridge Wells town centre which held a big attraction, not only for me, but also for teenagers and a few adults. The rock was dark grey in colour and had a surprisingly smooth surface. When I reached out to hold it it felt like I was grasping an unpolished apple. There were footholds everywhere because the rocks had been climbed so often by so many people. The footholds made climbing the rocks easier, unless of course you got your foot stuck in one of them. We would go to the rocks on a Saturday or Sunday afternoon, always accompanied by a member of staff or one of the older kids, never on our own. I liked playing on the rocks because every time I went there, there was always a new part to be conquered or discovered.

John and I shared a large bedroom in Domaris. The bedroom had three beds in it although only the two of us slept there. We had a chest of drawers and a wardrobe each. We went to bed at a set time every night, and like other young children John and I weren't eager to go to bed. At bedtime we would seldom go straight to sleep: we viewed it as a time for messing around, not for going to sleep. Jenny often found us in a full-blown pillow fight when she opened our bedroom door. Pillow-fighting was great fun until we discovered a new game: jumping off the wardrobes.

One evening after bedtime, John climbed on top of one of the wardrobes, which was on the opposite side of the room to his bed. Just then we heard Jenny's voice. As she opened the door John flew off the wardrobe. Jenny told us off for messing about and told John not to climb on the wardrobe because it was naughty and he would end up hurting himself. When she had gone I wanted to have a go myself. After plucking up the courage I made my first jump. Not only was it easy but it was much more fun than pillow-fighting. From that night on jumping off the wardrobes on to our beds became a regular activity.

Another bedroom antic that I recall was the sticky paper episode. I had been given some brightly coloured sticky paper as one of my birthday presents. I had not found a use for it and the paper had laid around for weeks after my birthday when one night an idea came to me. As soon as it came into my head I suggested it to John. We both agreed it would be funny if we put the sticky paper on the ceiling. I went and fetched it and we set to work. We had managed to stick about four pieces of coloured paper on the ceiling when in walked Jenny. I don't think she could believe her eyes. We were caught red-handed. She went spare and started shouting at us and telling us what a stupid thing it was to do. Later on that evening Peter came to our room to speak to us about our behaviour and the sticky paper on the ceiling. Although John and I got into trouble we still thought the whole incident was highly amusing. But what amused us most was that when the staff removed the sticky paper, one piece was left behind. This one piece stayed there for a very long time. So whenever we looked up at the ceiling we would collapse into uncontrollable giggles because there, in the corner of our bedroom ceiling, was this last piece of red sticky paper, a symbol of how mischievous we were and proof that we had had the last laugh.

When I was young the dustcart and the men who emptied the bins fascinated me. The refuse collectors came to St Christopher's once a week. I don't know why they fascinated me: perhaps it was the grimy clothes they wore. I can remember thinking to myself how very dirty they were, and that if I was to get half as dirty as that I would have been made to go indoors and have a thorough wash. The dustcart looked huge and monstrous and I wasn't keen on venturing too near it. In a strange kind of way I saw it as a dangerous prehistoric animal which thrived on rubbish. I thought if anyone was to fall into its mouth the big crushing jaws would come down and gobble them up. Although I liked watching the dustcart eating the rubbish and the dustmen working I never got too close to them.

One school holiday, John and I were playing near the driveway when the dustcart pulled in. I thought it would be interesting to watch it as I didn't often get to see it in action. I had been monitoring the goings on for a few minutes when John came up. In his hand he had about six rusty nails of various sizes. He explained what they were for: his plan was to strategically place the nails in the middle of the driveway and see what would happen. Because the tyres on the dustcart were so massive John wanted to see if the nails could be embedded in the tyres without causing a puncture, or whether the dustcart would get a flat tyre. I didn't want anything to do with this as I was afraid of what might happen if it did get a puncture.

John eventually persuaded me to help him put the nails out in the drive ready for the dustcart. He reasoned that if it did get a puncture we wouldn't be in trouble because it was just one of those things and nobody would think we had placed the nails there deliberately. After positioning the nails on the driveway we stood nearby, waiting for the cart to finish its round and come past us on its way out. As it approached the nails I was feeling quite nervous. Suddenly it was all over. The dustcart was heading out of the drive. The rubbish-eating monster was triumphant: not one single nail went in. Afterwards we counted them and they were all there. I was very relieved that nothing untoward had happened, but I'm not sure John felt the same way.

Jenny and Peter took some of us on holiday to Greatstone-on-Sea on the Kent coast. I have only patchy memories of this holiday although there are two details about the house we stayed in that still remain sharp in my mind. First was the number of front doors the house had: three. I can remember thinking how odd this was and wondering why. Peter said it was something to do with security. The other thing I remember is the lack of bedrooms. The problem was resolved by putting an extra bed on the landing at the top of the stairs. I didn't like the look of it one little bit because there didn't appear to be much in the way of protection. If you fell out of the bed in the night you had a good chance of ending up at the bottom of the stairs. I wasn't the only person who didn't relish the idea of sleeping in that bed, and in the end we took it in turns to sleep in it.

This was to be the last holiday I was to spend with Jenny and Peter, and I am lucky enough to have in my possession some photographs from it which keep alive memories of those happy days. My life and the 'family' I had always known was about to start changing, and the first wrench was already on the horizon.

I had grown up with Clare, who lived in Domaris, from a young baby. We were very fond of each other and enjoyed each other's company. I remember us spending many hours talking and playing together and we were the best of friends. She was my first ever girlfriend. We were very young at the time, but we were definitely in love. It is extremely difficult to put the relationship into words, but even at that age my feelings for her were different from the brotherly feelings I had for the other girls in the house.

One day it was announced out of the blue that Clare would be leaving St Christopher's to go and live with her mum in London. Of course Clare and her elder sister were pleased to be going home to live with their mum, but as the day of her departure got closer and closer I became more and more anxious about it. On one hand I knew it was good that she was going home to her real mum, but on the other I realised that I would miss her very much and I didn't like the idea of being in St Christopher's without her.

On the eve of Clare's departure I kept remembering that by the next evening she would no longer be living at Domaris. I felt awful but tried to put on a brave face. Our last evening spent together was a warm summer's night. We talked for hours that night, and it was all very emotional. We talked about things we had shared together and of our everlasting love for one another. After our lengthy talk about the past and a little bit of the future, we decided to have a farewell kiss. Although we had been in love for some time we had never kissed each other. After all, we were both only six at the time and until now our physical contact with one another had consisted of holding hands. For our farewell kiss we went and hid behind a semi-circular stone wall. We slid down the wall until we were in a crouched position and then we kissed. I have always treasured that precious moment in my life. This was my first kiss from my first ever girlfriend.

The next day Clare left St Christopher's and I never saw her again.

John had made friends with a boy who lived on the other side of St Christopher's. His name was Ron Mayor, and his mother, Angela, worked as a house mother. John started going over to see Ron regularly and before long they had become good friends. I didn't take much notice of the fact that John was spending more time with Ron until it got to the stage when I hardly saw him at all. Then I began to wonder what John could be doing all this time. One day I was told that John, too, would be leaving Domaris, to move into the Mayors' house on the other side of St Christopher's. He liked Ron, and the house parents agreed that John could move in. John spent so much time over there that he practically lived there anyway.

My initial reaction was one of pure jealousy. How could he want to go around with Ron rather than me? I thought long and hard about the situation and came to the conclusion that it wasn't worth making a big fuss. John had obviously made up his mind and that was that. However, in the back of my mind a doubt lurked. Why did John want to go around with Ron? What was wrong with going around with me? I never did find out the answer to my question. I was about six and a half when John moved out. His departure came quite soon after I lost Clare, and I felt very bereft. John and I were very good friends and had known each other all our short lives, and although he would still be living at St Christopher's I somehow knew that our relationship would never be the same when we were living apart. I was to be proved right. The day John moved out to the

Mayors' was a very unhappy day for me, but I had to put on a brave face once again. From this day on John and I were to grow apart.

I had been told a couple of months before their departure that Jenny and Peter were leaving St Christopher's to start a family of their own. I didn't give it much thought and I suppose I had tried to block it from my mind. But time had passed quickly, and suddenly it was tomorrow that Jenny and Peter would leave Domaris for good. I wanted to beg them to stay but I knew this would only make matters worse. I would have given anything for them to have taken me with them. It was only now that the harsh truth started to dawn on me with a brutal clarity.

Jenny and Peter were not my mother and father. They were going off to start a 'real family'. Knowing this didn't change my feelings at all – I still didn't want Jenny and Peter to go. I missed Clare badly, and John's defection had left me feeling hurt and left out, but this was really serious. Jenny and Peter leaving! I was devastated. My whole world had been destroyed.

I was not at school on the day Jenny and Peter left. It may have been the school holidays, for it was in the summer of 1971 that they left. Anyway, I was at home all day. The staff wanted to get Jenny out of the house so that they and the other children could play tricks on her. It was a tradition to stage pranks on house parents when they left. That day there were lots of hoax phone calls for Jenny, which sent her on all sorts of unnecessary errands around St Christopher's. Meanwhile, back at Domaris, the staff and some of the children were filling Jenny's and Peter's shoes and pockets with sticky and messy things from the kitchen. I didn't play tricks on Jenny and Peter and wanted the others to stop. They thought it was fun; I thought it was horrible. I failed to see the funny side of it at all – to me there could be nothing amusing about Jenny and Peter leaving. Sending Jenny on these bogus errands meant that she was out of the house when she would have otherwise been there, so her last few hours at St Christopher's were patchy and disrupted. It only made matters worse on an already dreadful day.

At about midday, Jenny and Peter said their farewells to all of us and left.

An hour or two later the new house parents, Mr and Mrs Mitchell, were on their way to Domaris. Everyone gathered dutifully in the hall when the Mitchells arrived. There they all stood like a waiting committee, their curiosity getting the better of them. I wasn't there to greet the Mitchells. Who were these strange people coming to take over the house? I didn't want to look but I needed to know. On entering Domaris, the Mitchells said hello to everyone in a general manner and later to us all individually, accompanied by a staff member to introduce them.

The Mitchells were a fairly young couple with two children of their own, a young daughter of three and a baby boy. Vivienne, the mother, was a petite woman with black shoulder-length hair and a friendly face. Patrick was of medium build and not very tall. He had fair hair and a stern face. The daughter Denise was a pretty but watchful little child. Her brother, Louis, just a baby, had white wispy hair.

From the moment the Mitchells stepped into Domaris I instinctively knew my childhood was over. I can't explain the feeling but it filled my whole body and mind. When I saw Patrick Mitchell my feelings were confirmed. The good times were now consigned to history. I just knew it. I don't know how, I just did. In a few short hours my whole life completely changed and it would never be the same again. This day was to be the worst day of my life. Never had I experienced these feelings before, and although I was only seven years old, somehow I felt I was no longer a child. After the formalities and introductions were over, the Mitchells started bringing in their belongings. I felt ill, for their belongings symbolised one important thing: permanency. I knew there was no going back, and the Mitchells were there to stay.

# PART II

# 4

# A Living Hell

Not long after Patrick and Vivienne moved in, new children started to arrive. Of course Domaris had vacancies now that John and Clare had moved out. The new children who moved in were all girls. The twins were younger than I and there was another very young child called Tanya, who was backward and had been physically abused by her parents. I felt pity towards Tanya and always felt disgusted when the evidence of her abuse caught my eye. It always pleased me when I saw her making progress or enjoying herself. Seeing Tanya smile never failed to cheer me up. I never really got to know the twins very well although I lived with them for some time, but we weren't unfriendly towards one another. Being twins, they were pretty wrapped up in each other.

Within days of the Mitchells' arrival the situation between us had become an 'us and them' confrontation.

Patrick and Vivienne had not lived in Domaris long when the live-in helper moved out. Her replacement, Debbie, arrived shortly afterwards. Debbie was tall and had a friendly, approachable look about her. Although she had come to work at Domaris after the Mitchells I didn't feel that she was as much of an intruder as they were. I liked her and got on well with her, but I wouldn't say we were close friends. I didn't really approve of Debbie being so close and friendly with the Mitchells – I suppose I saw it as a betrayal. I would have liked Debbie much more had it not been for that. But, overall, we got on quite well.

Usually I walked to and from school with the other children

from St Christopher's, or sometimes on my own. One afternoon Patrick picked me up in the car, along with some of the other children who went to another school. We all drove to Denise's school to collect her. As we left we passed a lollipop man. Patrick asked me what it said on the lolly.

'Stop.'

'How do you spell it?'

'S-T-O-P,' I replied.

Patrick then asked me to spell the other word on the lollipop. I hadn't seen the other word because it was on the other side, but before I could explain this Patrick's daughter said 'Children,' and spelt it out, 'C-H-I-L-D-R-E-N.'

Patrick looked at me vindictively and said, 'Right, you're getting a spelling test when we get home.'

My heart sank. I didn't like spelling much, nor did I like the look on Patrick's face, nor the tone of his voice. For the rest of the journey home I sat agonising over the forthcoming test. As we got nearer and nearer Domaris a feeling of impending doom descended upon me. We had been back in the house only minutes when Patrick announced that it was time for my spelling test. This was after he had told the whole house that his daughter was better at spelling than I was, putting a lot of emphasis on the fact that she was four years younger than me.

Patrick started off with the word 'thee'. This was a word I hadn't heard before. I knew the word 'the', but 'thee' really threw me. 'Thee, thee, thee, come on, spell it,' he insisted. I wasn't sure of this word so I said nothing. 'It's easy,' Patrick said. 'You must be able to spell "thee".'

On hearing this I decided not to say anything because if it was that easy and I got it wrong it would cause me more trouble and humiliation. Patrick persistently hounded me. 'Come on, spell "thee".' This relentless nagging went on for some time; it seemed like hours. Eventually he gave in. He had had enough of my wall of silence. He said the spelling test was over. I felt a sudden release. But then he said that I had to go to bed and go without tea. I went up to my room feeling dejected, humiliated and helpless. Yet in one way I was glad to be upstairs alone – at least Patrick wasn't there. Nevertheless, I resented being deprived of my tea just because of his nasty spelling test.

Later that evening when the other children came to bed a couple of them came in to see me. They said they were sorry I'd had to go without my tea, but they wanted to know if it was true that I couldn't spell the word 'the'. I couldn't believe it. 'The'! He had said 'thee'! I explained what had happened, that because of the way Patrick had pronounced it I thought it was a different word. I thanked them for their information. Now I was seething with anger. That horrible Patrick had conned me and made me go without my tea. It was a nasty trick to play on me, saying 'thee' instead of 'the'. Of course I knew how to spell 'the'. I wasn't good at spelling, but I could easily spell 'the', if only Patrick had pronounced it properly.

One day I came home from school with a button missing from my coat. Thinking little of it I hung up my coat as usual. A few days later a helper noticed that my button was missing, and after tea Patrick took me into the cloakroom to speak to me about it. After much lengthy questioning – how did I lose it? Where did I lose it? Why hadn't I told someone about it? – Patrick decided that I should sew on a new button. He made it clear to me that sewing on the button would serve as recompense for my wrongdoings. I was given a needle, cotton and a button. It took me a long time to thread the needle. I didn't tie a knot in the end because I didn't know anything about sewing. I laboured long and hard over the sewing, alone in the cloakroom. By the time I had finished, there, on the tip of the button, was a mound of loosely woven black thread. It looked like an extremely ill-fitting wig perched upon a large, flat head. When I turned my coat upside down it stayed on. I was filled with a sense of achievement although it had taken me a couple of hours to get even that far. Yes, I had done it! The button stayed on!

I was feeling glad that the job was over when Patrick came along and asked if I had finished. I said yes, feeling quite pleased with myself. Patrick took the sewing from me, looked at it and, with the coat in one hand, he placed his other hand over my sewing. Then he plucked off the button just as if he were picking a blackberry from a bush. I looked at him with awe. I had done all that hard, painstaking work only for him to come along and do that.

Patrick said to me: 'You're not very good at sewing, are you?'

I thought I had done quite well, but I replied: 'No, I'm not.'

He told me to take my coat to Debbie and ask her nicely if she would please sew a button on my coat.

When it was felt by member of staff or Patrick and Vivienne that I had done something wrong, Patrick would punish me. One of his favourite punishments was to make me stand and stare at a wall for hours on end. I can't remember exactly for what misdemeanours this punishment was dealt out, only that it was a regular occurrence. First I would be made to stand in front of a wall, about one or two inches away from it. I would be told not to move or talk to anyone, nor was I allowed to move my head to look at anything other than the wall in front of me. The duration of this punishment was anything from twenty minutes to a matter of hours. Sometimes, for added punishment, I would have to put my hands on my head at the same time. If I wanted to go to the toilet I would have to ask special permission from Patrick. This penance was dealt out to me many times, but one example that sticks in my mind happened at Christmas. I always hated this punishment, no matter how long or short its duration. I hated standing still all that time, but most of all I hated the boredom. It practically drove me to tears. When I had to stand staring at a wall during the festive season it was a bit more bearable in some ways and made me even angrier in others. The Christmas cards on the wall helped to relieve the monotony, but while they helped the time to pass until I was told I could go to bed, I couldn't help feeling that the Mitchells wouldn't have received half as many cards had the senders known what Patrick was really like.

One Sunday morning a man and a woman came to visit Julie, the deaf child. They said they would like to buy all the children some sweets and comics and they wanted to take one of us with them to the shops to help choose what the other children would like. Patrick and Vivienne agreed to let me go to the sweetshop. By the time we got there I had already told the people what the children's favourite sweets were, so I expected to be left to wait in the car while they went and bought all the goodies. But they got out and then opened the door for me. I didn't need any further prompting and jumped out straight away. Once inside the shop I was told by the two adults to go and choose some sweets. I soon came back to them clutching lots of brightly coloured confections.

I put them on the counter as I was told, and the mound of sweets grew higher and higher. Most of them were for the other children because I knew they all loved sweets; only a small part of the mound had I set aside for myself. The grown-ups then asked me to select some comics for the other children and one for myself. This I did as best I could, but choosing comics for everyone was more difficult than choosing sweets. By the time I had finished you could hardly see the counter for sweets and comics. The grown-ups paid the shopkeeper, and I think the bill came to about six or seven pounds.

Back at Domaris I sat down to eat some sweets and look through my comic. I could tell from what they were saying and the looks on their faces that the other children were delighted with what we had brought back for them. My own thoughts were occupied by the reactions of the other children and my own comic and sweets so I wasn't aware that Patrick and Vivienne were taking a dim view of the whole enterprise. They thought that I had been exceedingly greedy and had wheedled all these sweets and comics out of the visitors. Until Julie's friends had gone I was totally unaware of their displeasure about what I was supposed to have done.

As soon as Julie's friends had walked out of the door Patrick and Vivienne started telling me off. I didn't understand why. 'Why did you get those people to buy so many sweets?' they said. 'You're a greedy little boy,' and 'You know you shouldn't have done that.' I could tell by the tone of their voices that no matter what I said in my defence it would be to no avail. Then they confiscated my sweets and told me that I would not be allowed to have any more for the next six months. This punishment probably did my teeth the world of good, but emotionally I felt I was the victim of yet another injustice.

About three weeks later a woman visited Domaris and asked Vivienne whether she could hand a sweet round to all the kids. Vivienne said she could as long as she didn't give me one because I wasn't to have sweets. She explained that I had been a greedy boy and how I had tricked other visitors into buying me lots of sweets. The anger and resentment I felt towards Patrick and Vivienne took root. I wasn't concerned about going without sweets – that I had got used to – but telling horrible lies about me and humiliating me in front of visitors I really objected to. But I was unable to say or do anything about it and I just had to take it as best I could.

In spite of my feelings of foreboding when Patrick and Vivienne took over Domaris I hadn't had any conception of just how much of the old life was going to disappear. Within a month, or even weeks, I had found out the hard way. The one constant factor was Julie. She, like me, had been living in Domaris for years. We got on well, we had grown up together and we were roughly the same age, and so Julie and I joined forces. Although she was deaf we managed to communicate somehow, using official and unofficial sign language. We spent quite a bit of our free time together. It gave us both a feeling of security and a certain amount of protection. Julie and I shared whatever we had, sweets and other little treats. Whenever either of us got into trouble we would always try and stick up for one another. If we both got into trouble, then we would just console each other.

Patrick and Vivienne both smoked, a habit which was new to me as neither Peter nor Jenny had been a smoker. Within a month of the Mitchells' arrival I had the desire to try a cigarette because I thought smoking was a thing grown-ups did. But I had no money to buy cigarettes. I thought of taking one from the Mitchells' packets, but decided against this idea as it was very risky. I later came up with a foolproof plan: I would look for a longish discarded cigarette butt on my way back from school. A few days later I found a really big cigarette butt, and in the evening I tried to smoke in my bedroom. At the time I had a small bedroom of my own. It had an electric heater which I used to light the cigarette. Once I had got it alight I took only a few quick puffs before I heard footsteps. I quickly threw it out of the window and was just waving my arms around to get rid of the smoke when Denise walked in. She had come to say goodnight. When she left my room after telling me to close the window, a feeling of relief came over me. Somehow I had got away with it.

From quite an early age I realised that I lived in a children's home, and that Jenny and Peter weren't my real parents. But this didn't have much of an effect on my life while Jenny and Peter were there as my substitute parents. When Patrick and Vivienne moved in, it heightened my awareness that I was in care and did not have a real mum and dad. The misery I felt now because of the events that were taking place at Domaris kindled a strong desire for my natural parents. I now desperately needed my own mum and dad, but I knew nothing about them, not even their names. I hadn't seen a photograph of them so I had no idea what they looked like. No one had ever told me anything much about my mum and dad. But for some reason I knew they were alive; had I been told they were dead I would have remembered it. When I was very young someone must have explained something about my parents to me, for I was sure they were living. I remember asking questions about where they were, and when they were coming to see me. I was always given short and inadequate answers to my questions.

The staff did not encourage me to ask or talk about my parents, and whenever I tried to discuss the matter with them they would quickly change the subject. I was desperate to know more, but because I was so young adults would dismiss and underestimate my increasing awareness about the existence of my parents.

At weekends the parents of the new children began to visit. This came as a surprise to me. Having other children's parents in Domaris seemed quite alien. I began to realise that my own parents had never visited me there. I had no recollection of visits during my first year in care. None of it made sense to me. Why didn't my mum and dad visit me? Why, why didn't they visit me? I kept asking myself this question but I could never come up with an answer. Every time the parents of the new children came to see them I felt isolated, unwanted, rejected and at the constant mercy of others.

In the summer of 1972, we all went on holiday to Cornwall and Devon. Generally speaking I enjoyed the holiday. We stayed at a cottage in Cornwall and in a farmhouse in Devon. While we were staying at the farmhouse there were a couple of rainy days so we stayed in. One evening I was in the sitting-room next to the kitchen, where I could hear Debbie and Vivienne talking. They were discussing putting together holiday scrapbooks for us children. After they had decided what sort of things they would include in the scrapbooks they then talked about which children to make them for. I heard them say: 'We won't do one for Fred. He's too old, and anyway he wouldn't appreciate it.' I could hardly believe my ears. What did they mean, I wouldn't appreciate it? I would have loved to have had a scrapbook of my holiday, something to add to my meagre collection of treasures recording my life. When I saw Debbie and Vivienne putting together the scrapbooks I didn't let on that I had heard their conversation. At the end of the holiday Vivienne and Debbie gave out the scrapbooks to all the children except me. I was jealous of the other children, even though I knew it wasn't their fault, and I felt horribly left out. Throughout the whole episode I put on a brave face. Nobody but me knew how hurt I had been about the holiday scrapbooks.

The staring at walls wasn't the only punishment Patrick dealt out to me. He also smacked me. The smacks came in various degrees of severity from hard, to very hard, to extremely hard. Most of these blows fell upon my legs, although occasionally he smacked me around the head. The severity of the smacks didn't really bear any relation to the seriousness of the supposed misdemeanour but depended on what sort of temper

Patrick was in at the time. I was hit fairly often. I always felt most vulnerable when wearing shorts. Long trousers didn't cushion the blows, but psychologically I felt happier wearing long trousers. When you were wearing shorts the smack always left a horrible and very visible bright red mark, a perfect imprint of Patrick's hand upon your leg. Patrick's handprint would often outlive the pain of the initial smack. I hated the mark more than the pain from the blow. The bright red brand on my pale white skin was a symbol of my helplessness, and of a life lived at the mercy of others. Whenever I wore long trousers it didn't feel quite as bad. The badge of my powerlessness was then not apparent to the naked eye.

I have very clear recollections of one of Patrick's interrogations. By some misfortune I managed to lose my coat; I don't know how or where. I told one of the staff that I had lost it and couldn't find it anywhere. That evening Patrick asked to see me in the cloakroom. I knew instantly why he wanted to speak to me. In the cloakroom he started to question me. Where had I lost my coat? What day had I lost my coat? When had I last seen it? On and on went the barrage of questions, most of which I couldn't answer. I told him: 'I don't know where I lost my coat and I don't know what day I lost it. The last place I saw my coat was in the cloakroom.'

'Whereabouts in the cloakroom did you last see your coat? Which peg was it on when you last saw it?'

I thought for a while, then pointed to the far end of the row of pegs and said 'Over there.'

'Which peg over there?' Patrick placed his hand on the four end pegs, stopping on each and asking 'This peg? That peg? This peg?'

Eventually I nodded and said, 'That one.' He looked around at me, his hand still on the peg, and said, 'Right, we'll look to see if it's here, then.' He removed the coats one by one and presented them to me, each time expecting me to confirm that the one he held out was mine. I knew my coat wouldn't be among them because I had already thoroughly searched the cloakroom. Patrick was clearly angry that none of the coats he showed me was mine. I suppose he thought I had just mislaid it, put it down somewhere without remembering where.

This definitely was not the case. I had lost my coat and there were no two ways about it. I wouldn't have dared to say I had lost it if there was any possibility of me finding it. I had searched everywhere at school before going home and telling a member of staff. It was the last thing I wanted to do for I could anticipate Patrick's over-zealous reaction.

He replaced the coats on the peg and said to me: 'Are you sure you last saw your coat on that peg?' His question made me think for a moment. I hadn't seen my coat for a few days. I might well have seen my coat on any one of several pegs.

'It might not have been that particular peg,' I replied.

'It might not have been that *particular peg*?' said Patrick in an unnatural posh voice, putting a lot of emphasis on the words 'particular peg'.

Then he went on and on, saying things like, 'Oh, not that *particular peg*,' 'Perhaps it was this *particular peg* or that *particular peg*?' He kept up the silly posh voice and made a lot of the words 'particular'. Listening to Patrick's reaction to what I had said left me bewildered. Why was he reacting like that? Going on and on in that silly voice and saying again and again 'that particular peg'? Being only eight at the time it made no sense to me at all. Patrick had turned his attention from the lost coat and was now concentrating on the words 'particular peg'. Eventually the interrogation drew to a close and I was sent to bed. That night I lay in bed trying to work out what had really gone wrong that evening.

All the children at Domaris had their duties to do in the evening when they came in from school. One of my tasks was to clean everyone's shoes. The shoe-cleaning took place in the cloakroom where the shoes where kept. After tea I would help with the washing-up and then go and do everybody's shoes. I didn't enjoy putting my hands into other people's smelly shoes. There were about eight pairs to clean and they weren't all the same colour. I became quite good at cleaning shoes though, through so much practice. Although I disliked it I took pride in the job. If the shine wasn't good enough Patrick would make me do them again and I hated this, so eventually I became an expert.

I cannot remember precisely when or in what order all these events took place, but they are so heavily ingrained on my mind that they still haunt me day and night. It all happened during the time I spent with the Mitchells, from 1971 to 1974, when I was between seven and ten.

During this time I moved from the small bedroom I had had to myself since John had left to sharing one with David. David had been at Domaris since the Coles' time, but as he was older than me – seven or eight years – I hadn't had much to do with him and didn't know him very well. He stood over six feet tall and was enormously built for his age. He was capable of putting the fear of God into men much older than himself.

From the outset I felt uneasy about sharing a bedroom with someone I didn't know, especially someone who was almost grown up, but being a mere child I had no say in such matters. The bedroom David and I shared was a large, square room painted in a light blue colour. The beds, which had once been bunk-beds, were diagonally opposite each other. In the other two corners were the door, and across from the door a hand-basin with a small mirror above it. Next to the door was my bed. David's bed was parallel to the sink. Being so young I would be sent to bed considerably earlier than David. His bedtime was something like 10.30 or maybe even eleven o'clock.

During the first few weeks I shared the room with David nothing unusual or untoward happened, but for some inexplicable reason things changed. I was no longer left to sleep in my bed peacefully. David, when coming to bed, would open the door and switch on the light and somehow it always seemed much brighter than normal. Once I had been woken up by the light I became restless, and would turn over to try to shut it out. David, half undressed ready for bed, would then make his way over to my bed, pull back my covers and order me out of bed. I complied, trembling with fear. David then took down my pyjama trousers and touched and fondled my genitals and backside. He would then tell me to put my pyjamas back on and go back to bed. This pattern was repeated a few times before things took a turn for the worse.

After waking me and putting me through this horrendous sexual abuse, sometimes while I was still in bed, David would then make me fear for my life. Although at the time I didn't understand what was happening, I was afraid of going to bed at night, and of the inside light going on, for this signalled terror. From the deadly pale whiteness of my face and my uncontrollable trembling limbs it must have been plainly obvious to the rapist that I was absolutely terrified of him.

He made me fear for my life by threatening me with castration. Each night, after assaulting me, he held me up in front of the mirror with one giant hand while roughly pulling my penis and testicles back underneath me with the other. The first thing I saw in the mirror was my pale and petrified face; then I would see David's hand where my genitals ought to have been.

'That's what you'll look like if you tell anybody.'

If this happened I would look like a girl. David made it perfectly clear that he would have no hesitation in carrying out his threats if I ever spoke a word to anyone about what he was doing. The threat of castration was always put across in the same way after the rapes had taken place. I was sure that his threats were real and there was no way I was going to try to prove otherwise.

Each night I would hope and pray that Patrick or Vivienne or Debbie might come in and catch him, but they never did. Every time I was hauled up in front of the mirror I wanted to die. I was too young to understand what dying was, but that was the feeling I had: I didn't want to be there, I didn't want to be anywhere, I didn't want to be. Whenever I have a flashback to those memories my mind always goes back to the mirror, and I recall his odious perspiration with such vividness that I become ill. It has been the cause of many sleepless nights.

The sleeping arrangements changed again, and I was enormously relieved to be moved out of the double bedroom and put once again into a small bedroom of my own. After the other room it was paradise. Yet my nights free from sexual abuse were numbered. I stupidly thought that being in a room of my own would protect me from David's sexual desires, but I had not been there long before David made the first of many uninvited visits. When I heard the floorboards on the landing creak and he came in I knew straight away that something bad was going to take place. And sure enough it did. He touched and played with my penis and testicles, as before, and this happened again and again.

Then one night David came into my room, woke me up and demanded that I put my hands on 'it'. I was petrified. After hearing David's demand for the second time, I gingerly brought out my hands from under the covers and did as I was told. It wasn't until many years later that I realised what 'it' was. On that terrible night David had had an enormous erection and had forced me to touch it.

Now when David invaded my room he didn't turn on the light for fear of detection, so instead of being scared when the light went on I was scared of the dark. He would spend only a few minutes there each time, probably because if he had been caught in my room it would have been difficult for him to explain what he was doing there. So at the end of each sexual assault I was no longer subjected to the mirror treatment. Yet this was by no means any consolation because the abuse went on relentlessly as before.

It is difficult to describe my feelings at that point. I was terrified that I would never be free of this living hell and that I would always be living in fear of David. There are no words in the English language that are capable of conveying the feelings of being a rape/sexual abuse victim, and it is impossible to truly express what my feelings were. The pain of rape/sexual abuse goes not only through your body and mind but reaches down into the depths of your soul.

One evening in early October I told Debbie, Vivienne and Patrick about the Hallowe'en party. Everyone in my class was going and it was to be fancy dress. During the next few weeks Debbie and Vivienne helped me make a fancy dress outfit. I ended up going as a pixie with big pointed ears. I hadn't asked either of them to help me to make my costume; Debbie and Vivienne both volunteered to help me. The weeks soon passed and I went to the party in my authentic pixie outfit. I enjoyed the party very much. The hall was hung with Hallowe'en decorations, we played Hallowe'en party games and there was plenty to eat and drink. The children had been allowed to invite parents if they wished and so there were quite a few of them there. Near the end Patrick and Vivienne turned up. They waited in the hall, watching all the parents and children enjoying themselves. When the party ended I walked out of the main door towards the exit to join them. I could tell by the look on their faces that something was wrong.

Before we had even reached the car Patrick and Vivienne were shouting at me. 'Why didn't you tell us that parents were invited?' 'Why didn't you ask us to come?' 'Why didn't you tell us?' 'Other parents were there!' The car ride home was very uncomfortable as both Patrick and Vivienne harangued me. Vivienne went on to remind me how much work she and Debbie had put into making my fancy dress costume. I never asked you to make it, it was your choice, I thought indignantly to myself. I knew that I was in for a heavy telling-off when we got back to Domaris. As soon as we arrived Patrick went straight in to tell Debbie what he and Vivienne had witnessed that evening. Debbie asked me why I hadn't invited her after she had put so much work into making my pixie costume. Then she and Vivienne went off to bed.

I was taken by Patrick to the cloakroom for further questioning. It was late in the evening and I had had a long exhausting day. All I wanted now was my bed. However, Patrick wouldn't let the matter rest. First he asked if I had enjoyed the evening. I said I had. He asked what I had had to eat and drink. I told him. Then he explained that he and Vivienne would have liked to have gone along to the party and that they had seen other parents enjoying themselves. Then it was back to the interrogation. Why hadn't I told them? Why hadn't they been invited? Why hadn't I told them parents were welcome? I kept silent. I was fully aware that parents were invited. I hadn't forgotten for one moment. The reason why I hadn't mentioned it to Patrick and Vivienne was because *parents* were invited. Patrick and Vivienne were not my parents and in no circumstances did I want them masquerading as my parents.

The party had been and gone and Patrick couldn't punish me by stopping me from going. So I thought that after this onslaught he would send me to bed, but there was more to come. He told me to stay where I was for a moment and went off, returning with a glass of water. He handed it to me and told me to drink it. It wasn't just water, it was salt water. Very, very salty water. After the first mouthful I handed the glass back. Patrick told me to drink it all. It was the nastiest thing I had ever tasted. Very slowly I drank the foul liquid, each mouthful tasting worse than the previous one. When I had finished there was a residue of salt in the bottom of the glass. Patrick took the glass from my hand, poured a little water from the tap into it and swished it about. Then he gave me back the glass and said, 'There's no getting out of it, you've got to drink it all.' As I took it I looked into his face and thought to myself, 'You evil man.'

I knelt by the bowl of the toilet next to the cloakroom feeling very ill. I started heaving. When the heaving motions began, Patrick said to me: 'Next time you go to a party you'll remember to invite us, won't you?' Then he left me alone to vomit. As I knelt, throwing up into the toilet, thoughts were going through my mind. 'You're not my parents, you're not my parents, my parents wouldn't do this to me.' I was angry. Patrick wanted me to invite him as my father. Although I had been punished I still felt I had done the right thing by not inviting them. They were *not* my parents.

I was not enjoying school much either. I can still remember primary school spelling tests. When we first started them I enjoyed them; it seemed like a fun challenge. However, it wasn't long before I changed my mind. When the teacher finished calling out the spellings we would exchange our papers with the person next to us. The teacher then called out the correct spellings and we marked them accordingly. Once that was over the papers would be switched back so you could see how you'd done. My spelling ability was very limited. On an exceptionally good day I could manage to get seven or eight out of twenty; usually it was more like four out of twenty or two out of ten. It was very embarrassing to get the lowest score in the spelling tests so I used to lie and pretend to have a higher score. The teacher became wise to the cheating, so instead of putting up our hands to show how many we had got right we had to write our name on the paper and hand it in. But I didn't mind not being able to cheat because telling the truth was not so embarrassing when you didn't have to do it in front of the whole class.

From about the age of seven I was sent out of various classes for talking, shouting, messing around or not paying attention. Outside the classroom my time was my own. I couldn't think of anything to do and would just stand around letting my imagination drift. When I told John about getting sent out and having nothing to do, he suggested going through the coat pockets. He made a point of doing so whenever he got sent out, he said, because you usually ended up with some profit to show for your bother. John told me that I would be surprised at how much money kids left in their pockets. Armed with this new information I now knew what to do to pass the time when I was sent out of the class. When it happened next I set to work as soon as the door closed behind me. Many of the pockets were disappointing, offering nothing but sweet wrappers. But about a third of them yielded a fruitful reward. Sometimes there were one or two sweets, sometimes a sizeable haul; other pockets contained a few pennies and occasionally I would find larger sums of money.

There is one coat pocket that I remember well. The coat belonged to a boy called Graham Jones. I knew it was his because written in small capital letters on paper bags containing some biscuits was his name: GRAHAM JONES. After I stole his biscuits once I thought he would never leave them in his pocket again, but when I was next sent out of the class Graham's biscuits were in the same place, in his coat pocket. During break time I overheard him telling his friends that his biscuits had gone missing, and that it had happened before. He checked with his mum and made sure that she had packed them. Yet every time I got sent out of the class I would nearly always search through the coat pockets to see if there was anything going, and I had to steal Graham's biscuits, in the little bags with his name on, quite a few times before he stopped leaving them in the cloakroom.

As well as rummaging through coat pockets I would also play tricks on the teacher from outside the classroom. In a corner of the corridor mathematical apparatus was stored. There were four-foot rulers, six-foot rulers and also metre measures on sticks. The trick was really good fun. It was difficult to keep quiet and to stop myself from laughing in anticipation. The trick had three parts to it. The first stage was to get the rulers and measures and carefully place them against the door. The second was to knock on the door a couple of times and the third part was to be hiding in the cloakroom before the teacher opened the door. If it worked effectively, the teacher who had sent me out would open the door and be showered with the apparatus. Meanwhile I would be in the cloakroom having a good laugh. It would be a very brief thrill, because the teacher would come and find me and make me put all the apparatus away, and give me a good telling-off into the bargain.

After I played this trick a few times the teacher became wise to it. If he needed to open the door when I'd been sent out for misbehaving he would always take the precaution of stepping to one side. He looked pretty stupid doing this on the occasions when all he found was some other teacher or a child with a message standing there. Even when he knew the rulers were there the trick still had the effect of disrupting the classroom. Once the door had been opened there was no stopping the apparatus crashing down upon the floor, making an almighty clattering noise.

At the age of eight I could just about cope with English. This must have gone unnoticed because the teacher started teaching us a foreign language: French. At first I liked this lesson. Learning how to count in French seemed interesting and different. However, as the lessons became more complicated I lost interest. The teacher would ask the children to read the French words from the blackboard. I became very despondent as I was unable to read French, especially under classroom pressure. The teacher often asked me to stand up and read from the board. I felt foolish and inadequate because I couldn't read the French correctly. After many embarrassing experiences I decided that I wouldn't do it any more. I had had enough of the French teacher taking every opportunity to embarrass me. One day I hid under a table in a bid to avoid having to read from the blackboard. I held in my hand a very long and robust poster tube. I just wanted to be left alone to re-emerge when the French lesson was over.

The lesson began with me under a desk. About ten minutes passed before the French teacher realised I was hiding there. When he did, he came over and asked me to come out. 'No. I'm staying here. I don't want to do your nasty French,' I said. The dialogue carried on for the next few minutes much as it had started, with the teacher asking me to come out and me defying him. After a while he lost his temper. He grabbed my jumper and pulled me from under the table. I had my back to him but as I stood up I manoeuvred the poster tube into position and with all my might whacked the French teacher around the head. The poster tube came down with quite a bit of force, for although I was quite young and small I had become very angry. For assaulting the French teacher I was given three whacks with the slipper by the headmaster. Although the slipper hurt I felt the French teacher got what he deserved for bullying me.

At the age of nine or ten I was still being sent out of classes for one reason or another. However, when I was sent out of the classroom at the top of the school building there wasn't much for me to do because there were no cloakrooms. Outside the room there was a library, and as I had no inclination to steal books I gave up pilfering on those occasions. Being sent out wasn't the only punishment dealt out to me, however. The two teachers in the open-plan double classroom had devised a unique punishment which I was given on quite a few occasions. It consisted of walking the full length of the large classroom with two encyclopaedias on your head. It was not a balancing act – you held the encyclopaedias in place with your hands. Sometimes I would spend the majority of the lesson walking up and down with books on my head. The punishment made my arms and head ache a bit, but in a way it was more fun than standing in a boring library.

The teachers at St Peter's Primary School had a habit of confiscating all sorts of things from children and putting the contraband in the drawers of their desks. One day I decided to regain what the teacher had taken from me during the lesson. What I planned to do was to sneak into the classroom when nobody was about and take from the desk what had been taken from me. It was lunchtime, and nobody was in sight as I crept into the classroom and made my way to the teacher's desk. Slowly I opened the drawer. Inside I found things that had been confiscated from other children as well as my own possessions. I was about to reclaim what belonged to me when in a flash I realised that if I took my contraband back, the teacher would have no difficulty working out who had been in her desk. I quickly decided to take some other confiscated things from the drawer instead, plus a small amount of money that was there, just lying around in the corner of the drawer.

That afternoon there was no mention of a robbery having taken place, so I thought I had got away with it. However, after I made another two, or possibly three raids on the teacher's desk it became apparent that she knew. One day, she said: 'There has been some stealing from my desk, and from now on it will be locked.' After a pause she went on: 'I would be grateful if the person who has been stealing from my desk would return the stolen property. The thief can return the items when nobody is in the room, so that he or she can remain anonymous.' I had no intention whatsoever of returning the stolen property. In any case, the sweets were all eaten and the money had long been spent. It was a shame that the teacher was locking up her desk, but I consoled myself with the fact that at least I hadn't been caught.

Ten minutes' walk from St Peter's school was a Spar grocery shop. We hardly ever went to the Spar shop because we used the handy corner shop right near the school. There was, however, a short period of time when the boys started to go down to the Spar after school. The reason for this was the arrival of football stickers featuring players from all the football clubs. The idea was to collect as many as you could until you had a full set. I didn't collect the stickers but I used them as currency to trade for sweets, sandwiches and money, or for a favour. The stickers were free from the shop, but you had to buy goods of a certain value to be eligible for the stickers. As I didn't have the money or the desire to buy anything from the grocery shop it was difficult to obtain the stickers, but along with a few other boys from school I soon found a way round the problem. The stickers were kept in a large open-topped container quite close to the door. We would wait until the shop looked fairly busy and then we would go in. Once inside we quickly filled our pockets with handfuls of stickers and then beat a hasty retreat. The mass pilfering of football stickers from the grocery shop went on for many, many weeks, until one boy got caught by the shopkeeper. I then thought it was a good idea to give up stealing football stickers, too.

The distance from St Christopher's to St Peter's school was quite short and I would walk there and back most days, unless the weather happened to be very bad. Sometimes I walked to school with other children from St Christopher's, or other children I knew, but most of the time I walked alone. When walking alone I was able to be alone with my thoughts. With other children I still had the same thoughts but I would be slightly distracted from them. The twenty-minute walk between home and school was about the only time I was free from abuse, trouble, aggravation or punishment. I never wanted to arrive at either destination, so I always took my time. On the way to school I'd think, I wonder what lessons I will be thrown out of today? But there was one thing to be said for school: it wasn't as bad as Domaris. As I got nearer and nearer school, I hoped that the day would go smoothly and that I wouldn't get into trouble. Yet trouble always seemed to come to me as if I were some kind of magnet.

Life had now become a never-ending, painfully harrowing assault course. The walk between school and Domaris was the walk between each obstacle. I would not have minded if the distance had been thousands of miles. The walk back to St Christopher's from school never failed to be a most horrendous journey. I knew that every step I took was a step closer to many painful hours of ill treatment in one form or another. I cannot put my innermost feelings about that treacherous walk into words, because the pain of those journeys went far beyond any words that can be written or spoken.

# 5

# The Three Bs

The Simons were a working-class family who lived in Sittingbourne. The family consisted of a father, mother and one son. The father's name was Bernard, the mother was called Betty and their son was Billy; the three Bs, Betty, Bernard and Billy. Bernard Simons was in his mid-forties or early fifties, a little man but very strong. He had extremely hairy arms and rugged hands. Bernard smoked twenty Embassy a day. He wasn't one for dressing up smartly and in a way his weather-beaten face suited his dress sense. His hair had seen better days for he was balding quite noticeably. He worked as a lorry driver, delivering and collecting scrap metal. He worked hard and seemed to enjoy his job.

Betty was in her early forties, and always had rosy cheeks no matter what the weather was like. I wouldn't say her face was unfriendly but it wasn't what you would call endearing. Betty had very little patience and a fiery temper, with which she ruled the household. She was a housewife and had set days for different chores. Her clothes were quite plain and simple, and she never went out without wearing a headscarf. Betty didn't smoke but she was very partial to sweets and chocolate.

Billy was twenty. He was a fairly tall, stockily built man with long curly hair and a pale face. He lived at home and always did what his mother told him to do, definitely a 'mummy's boy'. Billy's hobbies were cars, music, fishing and shooting. He worked as a car mechanic and loved his job – he had his own car and took great pride in it. Being an only child Billy could do no wrong. He took after his father in many ways for he too was a mild and quiet man.

The Simons wanted to foster a child, so they approached Dr Barnardo's. The family were investigated for suitability, and when all the necessary paperwork and interviews were over it was decided that I, Fred Fever, would be a suitable candidate for the Simons to foster.

One Sunday in January 1972 I was told to go and get washed and to put on my best clothes. When I came downstairs, all clean and smartly dressed, Vivienne informed me that some people were coming to visit me and would take me out that afternoon. When the strangers arrived they chatted with Patrick and Vivienne, and then they were introduced to me as the Simons. After we had a chat we all went out for the afternoon. I don't know where it was that we went, only that it was in the countryside. The weather was wet and overcast so we ate our picnic in the car. The whole experience was bizarre and mystifying to me: first I meet these strangers out of the blue, then I go off on a car ride with them, then I eat a picnic with them.

I remember that during the picnic Billy blew off and stank out the car. The smell was rancid and Betty and Bernard were clearly embarrassed. They wound down the windows to let in some fresh air and made comments to Billy about his bad guts. The whole episode only added to an already weird Sunday afternoon. During the journey back to St Christopher's there was a lot of talk about where they lived and about their house. Then the Simons started to talk about me going to their house for the weekend. As the events of that afternoon unfolded things got more and more bewildering. Once back at Domaris life went back to normal and I began to wonder whether any of it had really happened or whether it had all been a rather odd dream.

There were to be more outings on Sunday afternoons. I can't remember much about them, but I began to enjoy them more when I started getting to know the Simons family better. None of these later outings was as memorable or as surreal as the initial one.

The Simons lived in an old council house that backed out on to a railway line. There was a small front room, a living-room, kitchen and three bedrooms. There was no bathroom and the toilet was outside, halfway down the garden. On entering the house, directly in front of you was a long narrow passageway. The first room you came to was the cramped front room, stuffed with furniture and boxes. Further along on the left were the stairs leading to the bedrooms. The stairway was narrow, and instead of a handrail, a piece of rope had been fixed to the wall. Betty and Bernard slept in the front bedroom and Billy slept in the room opposite theirs. The third bedroom, a small box-room that overlooked the railway, was reached through Billy's room.

The living-room was where everything happened. In the corner under the window stood an old black-and-white television. A settee and some comfy chairs were grouped around the set and behind them stood the dining table and chairs. A coal fire heated the room and it was warm and comfortable. The kitchen was small and the amenities spartan. There was an old china sink with a cold water tap; if you wanted hot water you had to boil it on the gas cooker. There was little storage space, and other than a small table, a fridge and a water boiler there wasn't much in the kitchen. Outside was a small back yard. A tin bath which hung on a nail in the yard was brought into the kitchen for baths. Further down the yard, past the tin bath, was a coal shed and the toilet and then a gate that led to an alleyway. At the end of the yard there was a small bit of garden.

My first weekend at the Simons' started with a car journey to Sittingbourne. Billy picked me up from St Christopher's at about five o'clock and drove through villages, towns and countryside. The route was quite scenic and as all the places were new to me I found the journey absorbing. My head kept moving from one side to the other as I tried to make sure I didn't miss anything. I couldn't take enough in at once. It felt great being in the car and not knowing where I was going to finish up. By the time we arrived in Sittingbourne daylight had long since given way to the dark.

After Billy had parked the car he showed me to the house and knocked on the door a couple of times. Betty answered, beaming from ear to ear as she beckoned us in. I felt strange standing in the passageway. I had just casually walked into someone else's house. I followed Billy and Betty down the dim passageway into the living-room, where the only light came from the flickering of the television which Bernard was eagerly watching. He didn't speak. He was, as I was to discover, a man of few words. I wasn't in the living-room for more than a minute before I was told by Betty to come into the kitchen where she would make Billy and I a drink. After the darkness of the living-room the kitchen light seemed very bright. I had never seen such an old-fashioned place. The kitchen looked so primitive that I felt that not only had I travelled to a new place but also back in time.

While I drank my hot milk and ravenously ate the biscuits Betty had given Billy and me, Bernard came through the kitchen and started to talk to us. Then he went out again, returning promptly with a small object in his hand. It was a watch. As he wound it, he asked whether I had a watch. Then he gave it to me. 'It's got a cowboy on it . . . it's Hopalong Cassidy.'

At the bottom of the watch was indeed a small figure of a cowboy, with the words Hopalong Cassidy around it in tiny lettering. I was absolutely delighted. I thanked the Simons for the gift. After Billy and I had finished eating and drinking we all went and sat down in the living-room. When it was time for bed, Billy showed me to my bedroom. It all seemed like a minor adventure. Once I had snuggled in, Betty came to check everything was OK. She had explained about toilet arrangements, or rather the lack of an indoor toilet. If I wanted to 'go' in the night there was a 'potty' at the end of my bed.

I can't remember much else about my first weekend at the Simons, only that I was taken to see some of Bernard's and Betty's relations. The whole experience overwhelmed me so much that I wasn't really aware of what was going on. It was the first time since I was a baby that I had stayed with anyone not connected with St Christopher's and it seemed as if I had been picked up and put down on another planet. At the end of the weekend, late on Sunday afternoon, the Simons family drove me back to St Christopher's. It was very strange to have been away from Domaris for two days and then to go back. The weekend had been quite an initiation into a different way of life.

I looked forward to the weekends at the Simons'. They weren't perfect, but they were a damned sight better than being in Domaris.

Yet because the weekends didn't come around quickly enough or often enough, I used to get fairly anxious. When a weekend with the Simons was imminent I got very excited at the prospect of two whole days and nights free of physical and sexual abuse. One Friday afternoon I was so happy to be going away for the weekend that I nearly got myself killed. All day I had been thinking of the weekend to come. It felt such a relief to be going away. I came out of school that afternoon in a very jubilant mood and ran down the street as fast as my legs would carry me. I was in such a rush to get home that I forgot to stop at the main road. I ran straight out in front of a car. Luckily the driver managed to stop in time, but only just. There wasn't an inch between me and the car. I was physically all right but I felt pretty shaken up.

I hated going back to Domaris after a weekend away at the Simons'. The feeling of doom and gloom would start even before I got in the car to go back to St Christopher's. This feeling of uneasiness multiplied during the journey and the nearer we drove to the children's home the worse it got.

After a while it was arranged that I would spend the school holidays and every third weekend with the Simons. The weekends always started off with Billy collecting me from Tunbridge Wells and would always finish with me going round saying goodbye to Betty's and Bernard's relations, who always gave me some pocket-money. By the time I had said goodbye to them all I ended up with quite a haul.

As Billy had such a liking for cars he would often take me to banger racing, speedway, drag racing – and once to Brands Hatch. I was enthralled by it all: it was a hot, sunny day, and I watched eagerly as the cars roared past faster than I could turn my head to follow them. The racing cars were very noisy and so were the spectators: excitement buzzed as the chequered flag blew in the wind. I really enjoyed going to different places with Billy, seeing these fantastic, noisy cars. It made a thrilling day out.

The Simons family, especially Betty, were very keen on markets. Whether it was finding a bargain or whether it was the atmosphere I don't know, but over the course of these weekends I went to many open-air markets with them. Although I had no purchasing power I still took pleasure in looking round the market stalls. It seemed you could buy almost anything in the world there. I would have liked to have gone off and looked around the many colourful stalls on my own, but I kept close to Betty, on my best behaviour, in an effort to please the Simons.

One Saturday Billy took me to a football match. I am not sure who was playing or where the ground was, but I think it may have been Gillingham, which is the nearest League football ground to Sittingbourne. The match wasn't particularly interesting but listening to the crowd was. What I remember most was someone shouting the word 'shit'. That evening, when everyone was having tea, Betty asked me whether I had enjoyed the football match. I told her all about it and when I got to the part about the crowd shouting I said, 'Billy will tell you what they said.'

But before I could say any more Betty cut in: 'No, Billy's not allowed to use swear words either.' I slumped in my chair looking at Billy, as much to say what a mummy's boy you are, you can't even swear at your age.

Billy had his own portable black-and-white television set, which he watched in the evening in bed. I used to think that he led a charmed life – nothing ever seemed to go wrong for him. But one Friday night when I was snuggled warmly in my bed in the little bedroom next to his, Billy got out of bed to move the television. I heard him walking across the room when suddenly there was a loud crash. The handle must have given way. The television hit the floor with an almighty bang and Billy swore! Betty and Bernard came in to see what had happened and inspected the damage. Meanwhile I was under the covers laughing my head off; in fact I was laughing so much I thought that at any moment they might catch me. I couldn't help but laugh, though – it was the funniest thing that had happened in a long time. I had this urge, when it was all cleared up, to ask Billy 'What's on telly?' From that night onwards, whenever I wanted to have a laugh at Billy's expense all I had to do was think back to the television incident. I only had to think about it and I would be in fits of laughter.

After one weekend at the Simons' I came back loaded with booty from the relations. Altogether there was about £1.70. On the way back to St Christopher's I started plotting what to do with the money. I was now regularly in the company of smokers: Patrick and Vivienne smoked, so did Mr Simons, and I was convinced that smoking was an adult thing to do. My first attempt at smoking hadn't been what one would call successful, so this time I would do it properly. This time there would be no expense spared. I would buy some proper cigarettes. I gave the plan quite a lot of thought and came to the conclusion that I should buy the cigarettes from the grocer's shop as opposed to the corner shop near the school. By going to the grocer's shop I stood a better chance of getting served and also they didn't know me, as they did at the corner shop.

On the Monday morning on my way to school, I popped into the grocery. I asked the shopkeeper for ten No. 6 and a box of matches. The shopkeeper said: 'You're too young, I can't serve children.' I explained that the cigarettes were for my dad, who was at home with a bad leg and had asked me to come round and get them. The shopkeeper was quite taken in by my story, and he sold me cigarettes and matches. I wasted no time in getting out of the shop in case he asked awkward questions. A friend of mine was waiting outside the shop for me. He hadn't realised what I had gone in for but when I came out he was extremely surprised to see me clutching ten No. 6 and matches. As we walked excitedly towards school we planned to meet down in the toilets at break time, when we would open the cigarettes.

I spent the first lesson of the day thinking only of the interesting time ahead. As soon as the teacher announced it was break time I headed straight for the boys' bogs, as we called them. I was there only a minute or two before my accomplice came along. When all the other boys had been and gone I opened the cigarettes and handed one to my friend. After lighting our cigarettes we stood around posing, pretending to be very adult and stylish. After a few minutes of childish bravado we decided to finish our fags in the cubicles just in case someone caught us. I smoked only about three-quarters of mine because it made me cough and I threw the remainder down the toilet. When we came out of the cubicles we both said how much we enjoyed smoking. The truth was we hated the taste, but neither of us wanted to look anything less than tough so we had to put on an act. The place was full of smoke, so we got out of the bogs quickly before anyone came down and caught us.

In the small bedroom of the Simons' house there were lots of toys that had belonged to Billy when he was a child. After the first few weekends I was encouraged to play with the toys, and Betty told me to look upon them as my own. Billy was twenty and clearly had no further use for his old toys. I liked playing with them, especially the Action Man and all its gadgets. One day I was searching through the toys when I came across some Dr Who badges and one or two other interesting things. I liked them so much I decided to take them back to Domaris with me at the end of the weekend. I packed the goodies into my bag ready to take back. I thought nothing of it – after all, Betty had told me to think of them as my own. When packing the toys into my bag I thought, Billy isn't going to want to play with them over the next two weeks.

Sunday evening and it was time to go. When Betty carried my bag to the car she wondered why it was so heavy. She rummaged through it and found various articles that she deemed to be stolen. She brought the bag back into the house and started questioning me. Why were these things in my bag? I tried to explain as best I could that I'd thought the toys were mine to do what I liked with, but Betty wasn't having any of it. She was convinced that I was an ungrateful little thief who had tried to rob her. She made a real big thing of the incident and it was blown out of all proportion. The car journey back from the Simons' that weekend was very unpleasant – and not for the usual reason.

Betty was more angry with me than I had thought. I supposed after all the telling-off and shouting at me that she had finished disciplining me for the unthinkable crimes I was presumed to have committed. Nearly three weeks had gone by since the fiasco at the Simons before the staff came and told me that I wouldn't be going to the Simons for the weekend. Betty had said that my weekends at the Simons were to be suspended until she said otherwise. When I first heard the news my immediate reaction was one of sadness. I would no longer be able to escape from Domaris for a short break. No more abuse-free weekends. I would just have to put up with it, like I did the rest of the time. On reflection I thought I should have known it had all been too good to be true. Why should they care about me? I wasn't their child.

During the course of the next few months my memory of the Simons began to fade and eventually I almost forgot about them altogether. By this time I looked upon the weekends at the Simons' as a nasty trick that had been played on me. Hope had been dangled in front of me and then it had been snatched away without warning. It compounded my feelings of helplessness and the knowledge that I was entirely dependent on the whims of others. Then, out of the blue, I was informed that I would be going to the Simons for the weekend. I was astounded. Me, go to the Simons for the weekend? I had forgotten about them because I hadn't thought I'd ever see them again.

The first weekend back at the Simons', Betty gave me a mammoth lecture about stealing and my behaviour. I promised with as much sincerity as I could muster that I wouldn't 'steal' again. The weekend of my reinstatement coincided with the wedding of one of the relations. We all went along and I was taken round and introduced to yet more relatives. All the introductions began with: 'This is Fred. He's from Dr Barnardo's.'

The suspension was now lifted and I started going to the Simons' every third weekend as before, with Billy collecting me from St Christopher's. The visits seemed to go pretty much as before, except that the atmosphere had shifted slightly and Betty appeared to be keeping a beady eye on me. I had thought all was now well and that our differences had been sorted out. I had been punished, I had said I was sorry to Betty, and I was under the impression that the matter was now closed.

Yet it seemed that I was not going to be allowed to forget it. When the family drove me back to Tunbridge Wells on Sundays, Bernard would slow down going past Maidstone prison. Betty, sitting beside me in the back, would make a snide remark. 'That's where people get sent if they misbehave.' 'People get sent there for stealing.' 'In there you're locked up in a little cell.' Every weekend after the suspension the car journey home was the same. A nice, slow drive past Maidstone jail while Betty came out with a fitting comment. Sometimes during this part of the journey not a word would be spoken. Instead Betty would look at me and then look meaningfully towards the prison.

# 6

# Getting Away for a Break

In February 1974 I was sent to a special remedial school one day a week after my teacher at St Peter's said I needed extra help with my reading and writing. John was sent there too, and I was glad to have a chance to talk to him for I hardly ever saw him now that he had moved. But John and I had grown apart over the previous years and we were no longer as close as we had once been. Oddly, we were chauffeur-driven to and from the school in a gleaming black Bentley. The car was in immaculate condition, and the chauffeur always wore a cap. The remedial school itself was a rather strange place. The teachers were always very nice – I cannot ever recall them telling me off or punishing me. There were only five children altogether and two teachers. I don't know what I learnt there because all we seemed to do was art; we very rarely did boring things. Every week I went to the remedial school I did something I liked, or thought was interesting. There never appeared to be any pressure on me at the school and with hindsight I think I responded well in the special remedial environment.

One day I was working hard on a piece of brown lino with a Stanley knife when suddenly the knife slipped. Blood started to run rapidly from the forefinger of my right hand and within a couple of minutes it was everywhere. A teacher quickly ran to my aid with a bundle of tissues. I was taken to the casualty department of Tunbridge Wells Hospital, where a doctor cleaned up the wound and put in two paper stitches, which they called butterfly stitches. That evening when bathtime came I asked the staff what should be done about my finger, because I didn't want the dressing to get wet. Neither Debbie nor Vivienne had a solution to the problem. Then Patrick came up with an idea. I vaguely heard them discussing it. Debbie and Vivienne were saying: 'No, no, you can't put that on his finger.'

'It'll be all right,' said Patrick. 'It will keep the dressing dry.' At the time I had no idea what Patrick put on my finger. Only some years later did I realise that it was a condom.

Apart from cutting my finger I really enjoyed the time spent at the special remedial school. The only drawback was the stigma attached to going to a special school.

On 17 May 1974, one month before my tenth birthday, I went by coach on a school outing to London. We visited the Cutty Sark and took a boat trip up the Thames, and in the afternoon we had a look around HMS Belfast. While looking around the warship I got well and truly lost in the engine-rooms in the lower decks. It wasn't until it was time to leave the ship that anyone realised I was missing. In the end, one of the people who worked on the ship found me and reunited me with the school party. The adventure added to the excitement of the outing.

During the coach journey home I listened intently to the carefree chatter of the other children. It had been a great day and I was content. As we sped south, it came home to me that this wonderful day would come to an abrupt halt the moment I stepped off the coach. I thought about all that was happening around me and what was awaiting me once I got back. Whenever I enjoyed myself it only made returning to Domaris even worse. After a short deliberation, I decided that that evening I would run away from St Christopher's. I would go to my parents. I told a few of the children on the coach about my plan. I don't think they believed me. After the coach dropped us off at school, I walked home with another boy. When we got to St Christopher's I pretended to walk to Domaris, but instead I hid until he was gone and then returned to the entrance of the complex.

Dell Drive was the smaller of the two entrances. I stood there for some time, but thinking someone might come, I decided to hide. There were embankments on both sides of the drive and on top grew bushes and shrubs. At the top of the embankment I sat down behind a bush. I thought about my mum and dad and how glad they would be to see me after all these years. I had so much to tell them. Then I came to the conclusion that it would probably be better to wait until it got dark before moving. I had no idea what my mother or father looked like, or where they lived; I knew nothing whatsoever about them. An hour or so later I saw people looking for me, so I crouched down behind a bush. They began shouting my name. 'Fred! Fred!' Even though from where I was hiding I could see Debbie, who was calling me, my mind was made up. There was no way that I would give up the search for my mum and dad.

The warm summer evening seemed to go on and on. I heard and saw more people out looking for me. I decided to postpone going on the run until the morning as there were so many people trying to find me. Anyway, it would be easier in daylight. The hours drew on and eventually I fell asleep under the bush. The staff had notified the police of my disappearance and at 12.30am I was discovered by a young uniformed policeman. I was startled when I awoke to find myself looking into the face of the policeman, who had already picked me up in his arms. I was cold and stiff and disorientated. He took me to Domaris and I was given a hot drink and wrapped in a blanket. I was then taken to bed by Vivienne and Debbie. They sat on my bed for some time asking me why I had run away. I told them that I was going to find my mum and dad. Vivienne and Debbie wanted to know why I wanted to find them. I was far too scared of Patrick and David to tell them why I had run away. There was no way I could have told them how much I hated living at Domaris for I was sure that it would only have resulted in even more trouble for me.

The next day was a Saturday. The night before all the house fathers had been out searching the grounds of St Christopher's and the news that I had run away was all over the complex.

When I came downstairs for breakfast that morning there was an enormous crowd of children all wanting to know if I was coming out to play. After I had finished my breakfast I went outside with the children. None of them had really come to see if I was coming out to play, of course; they just wanted to hear some interesting details of my little escapade. My popularity with the other children had grown immeasurably overnight. I was a hero. But they didn't know that I had run away out of sheer desperation. Neither the children nor staff had any idea why I did it. How could I tell them that I was being physically, emotionally and sexually abused? That I had seen or heard nothing from my parents throughout my ten years of life and that I now desperately needed my mum and dad? I wasn't heroic, or tough, or hard or clever. I was an extremely vulnerable child trying to escape the painful life that had been forced upon me. My attempted escape was in vain, because for me there was no escape. Life carried on just as it had before.

In the summers of 1973 and 1974 I was sent on the Barnardo's camp, which provided a two-week holiday for young people with nowhere else to go on holiday. People from children's homes, foster homes, adopted children and any other young people who were in some way connected with Barnardo's were eligible to go. The person in charge of the Barnardo's camp was Jim Johnson, a social worker. He and three members of staff were in charge of us. The other children on these camps were a very mixed bunch of individuals from a variety of backgrounds; some quiet, some noisy, some rough and aggressive. Some were shy, although not many; some were sociable, others anti-social. Generally they were a decent crowd of people as long as you kept on their good side. I was nine when I went on my first Barnardo's camp. Other kids from St Christopher's also went, such as John, and Jerry Atkins, who was a right head-case. The people from St Christopher's were one of the first groups of children to be picked up by the bus, which was a massive ex-military hospital Bedford van. It was colossal. It had been converted and there were rows of uncomfortable black seats in it. We had the best choice of seats, unlike the last few to be collected, who had to make do with what space they could find.

The campsite we went to was a disused army barracks, not far outside Deal on the Kent coast. The site consisted of one long road, some swings, a check-point hut, a very large canteen, toilets, two wash huts (one for boys and one for girls) and about fifteen disused barrack huts. One could be forgiven for mistaking the accommodation for cowsheds. The furniture in the huts was very sparse; indeed, other than the bunk-beds, there was only a small locker which you shared with the person you shared the bunk-bed with. The washing facilities were OK, except that it was always a job to get hot water so you often had to have a cold shower. The campsite canteen was a massive, dingy building. A siren went off to let you know it was meal-time, and to get your food you had to queue up in a line. It was served on paper plates and paper bowls. The cutlery was normal metal cutlery and the mugs for the tea were plastic. After we had queued up for our food and sat down at a table the canteen staff would bring round enormous dark brown teapots filled with hot, rusty-coloured tea. It had so much sugar in it that it was like drinking syrup. On a good day in the canteen there might be a food fight, although I only saw a couple of these. The other children who used the campsite were from underprivileged and poor backgrounds, mostly from the inner cities.

Deal, the nearest town, wasn't at all lively – in fact it was a very small, quiet community village in Kent. There wasn't much to do there. All it boasted in the way of leisure amenities was a long row of shops and a few public houses. It was a very dull and boring place for kids. At night some of the older ones would sneak out and go down to the pub, which was a long walk from the campsite. Most nights they would come back drunk. One night I remember someone puked up outside the hut.

Another night-time activity the older ones got up to was burning the soles of your feet to see how tough you were and to see your reaction to a bit of pain. Apparently, some sleeping victims would merely move their feet, while others would scream out loud. The burning of feet was a favourite trick and was something of a tradition on Barnardo's camps. People who had their toes burnt one year would become toe-burners the next, and so the practice was perpetuated.

Some days we would be taken on some sort of outing, but if not, the staff just drove us down to Deal for the day. The most memorable trip for me was a visit to Canterbury to watch motorbike speedway on my second camp, which was a smashing evening. Whenever we got to our destination, Deal or wherever, Jim Johnson would dish out some pocket-money to the children. The way it worked was quite simple. On the first day of the camp you gave all your money to Jim, who would write down your name and the amount you gave him in his book. Then, each day when he dealt out the cash, he would deduct the sum from the total. This system made sure you didn't run out of money on the first day, and it meant you didn't have to keep an eye on your cash in case someone nicked it.

A high percentage of children on the Barnardo's camps were partial to stealing things and smoking. After Jim Johnson had dealt out the cash everyone would go their separate ways, and most of us would go round in groups or pairs. Some of these would become 'stealing parties', and some of their members were quite expert at what they did. Within a matter of a few days the little Kentish village had been well and truly turned over. Barnardo's children and the others on the campsite went through the village like a swarm of locusts. During the first week of the camp the local police made a raid on the campsite for stolen property. Apparently many locals, nearly everyone in the village in fact, were complaining to the police about the massive increase in stealing. However, we had been warned in advance about the raid so any stolen things we had were safely hidden by the time the police came to search the site. They found nothing in our part of the camp but they did arrest one person from the other group who was found in possession of some stolen property.

Over the two weeks there would be the odd fight between Barnardo's children and the other children on the site, and there were also a few among the children from Barnardo's. One night during the holiday there was a football match, Barnardo's versus the other children. I cannot remember now who won but I do remember that it was fought very fiercely and that football skills didn't really come into it.

The older children on the camp would get up to all sorts of pranks. One of these was to put up a dirty clothes line. They would rummage through everyone's clothes to find underwear with skid-marks on it, both boys' and girls'. Then they put up a line near the huts and pegged out all the underwear. The owners of the underwear got very embarrassed while all the others would have a good laugh at their expense.

A day trip which was organised every year on the Barnardo's camp was a visit to the White Cliffs of Dover. Dover isn't far from Deal so the journey didn't take long. It wasn't exactly exciting but it made a change from Deal. Other than slipping off the cliffs and breaking our necks you wouldn't have thought that us kids could cause any trouble up there, but some people can always find it. One year, as we were heading back to the bus to return to the campsite, we spotted a kiosk selling sweets and ice-creams. Some of us bought things there and some stole them. One of the kids nicked a stand of chewing gum, not just a packet but the whole bloody stand, and ran off. He gave us all a couple of packets each and we all sat on the bus trying to look as if nothing had happened while trying to contain our laughter. Jim Johnson boarded the bus and asked who had nicked the chewing gum. Nobody answered. The man in the kiosk knew it was one of us but didn't know which one. Jim went off and told the man that he didn't know who had robbed him. On the journey back to Deal somebody asked Jim if he would like a piece of chewing gum; then all of a sudden, he was bombarded with the stuff. He was pretty wound up by the afternoon's events, but he wasn't really angry with us.

During the two-week holidays I got to know lots of new children, some of whom I became good friends with. I particularly remember two black boys who were brothers, who became great friends with John and me. There were, of course, some kids on the camp that I didn't like, but I made more friends than enemies.

The second summer on Barnardo's camp we slept in tents instead of huts. We took the tents down to the site and the children helped put them up. The tent that I wanted to sleep in was full and there just wasn't room for another kid. Tent places were decided by fights. If you won the fight you stayed in the tent and the loser had to get out. So there I was in this tent laying into this kid so I could sleep in the tent. He didn't have much of a chance because I was sitting on his chest punching his face in, while some of the other kids who had goaded us into the fight were sticking in the boot. The poor kid at the bottom of all of this had absolutely no chance of winning. Eventually it was decided I was the winner and that I could stay in the tent.

Many of the children on the second camp had been there the previous year, so I was able to meet up with old friends I hadn't seen since then.

That year a group of Scouts were also camping on the site. As well as having tents to sleep in, they had a marquee where they often spent their evenings. At night when it was dark John and I, plus a few other kids from our group, would sneak over to the Scouts' tents and let them down. We did this about three nights running. Then one night a man chased us and yelled at us. We didn't stop running so he shouted that he was going to set the dogs on us. We didn't hang around to see the dogs. We just ran like mad, dived into our tents and quickly closed them up behind us. There was some more fun with the tents but it was mostly our group letting down each other's in the middle of the night. Eventually the novelty wore off and we were able to get some sleep.

John had suffered from asthma ever since he was born. He used an inhaler which he took everywhere with him, in case he needed it. One night he had a very serious asthma attack in the middle of the night. His inhaler did nothing to help his breathing, the attack got worse and worse and in the end he had to be rushed to the nearest hospital. That evening I couldn't sleep. I sat up waiting for news of John's condition. I was terrified that John, who was the closest thing I had to a brother, was going to die. I was in a pretty bad state and only when I saw John return from the hospital and knew that he was OK could I relax.

On the last night of the holiday there was a big bonfire and everyone sat around cooking. We talked around the crackling fire until late into the evening and a couple of friends and I started to really get to know one another. One kid told me that his brother was in prison for armed robbery. The brother was a security guard who had been paid by the robbers to turn a blind eye when the raid was staged. When he was caught by the police he got the same prison sentence as the robbers. We talked the whole thing over and at the end of our conversation he thanked me for being a good listener. I told him it was nothing, I had enjoyed and learnt from our conversation. I had learnt that life wasn't fair, and that the police didn't understand why people did the things they did. The teenagers on the camp seemed to distrust the police. I could now see why, and I also began to distrust them too.

By 1974 I was ten years old and I still didn't know who my real parents were. According to Barnardo's records they had come to see me a couple of times, but I have absolutely no recollection of this. The visits took place, apparently, during my first year in care. Apart from these early visits my mother and father had no contact with me. I was never sent birthday cards, Christmas cards, letters or even postcards from my parents. I never knew why they didn't visit me or write to me, but I still longed for them. Although I had never seen them I believed that some day they would appear and give me a wonderful, loving, caring home, something of which I had been deprived since Jenny and Peter left St Christopher's.

In December 1972 it had been agreed that I should be fostered by the Simons. They were waiting to be re-housed at the time, and they were rather fussy about the sort of house they wanted, which made the delay longer than anticipated. Throughout 1974 the Simons were holding out for a house with two living-rooms on the Manor Grove Estate.

On 24 December 1974 I at last left Domaris, St Christopher's, Tunbridge Wells to go and live with the Simons in their new house. My last hours at St Christopher's were very nerve-racking and I had a bad case of butterflies in my stomach. I couldn't wait, I just couldn't sit still that evening. I couldn't really believe I was leaving and I was worried that something would go wrong and I would be disappointed again. Eventually the Simons came to pick me up. What a relief! They had come! I said my goodbyes to everyone. I felt sad saying goodbye to Julie and a couple of the other children; I knew what it was like to be left behind. As the car drove out of St Christopher's I was filled with conflicting emotions. I was sad to be leaving all my friends, sad about leaving a place I had once loved so dearly. However, I felt glad to be getting away from David and Patrick and the painful years of physical, sexual and emotional abuse. I was also apprehensive about the future. What was it going to be like living with my new parents, the Simons? What was it going to be like in a new town with new people? What would my new school be like? My mind weighed very heavily throughout the car journey to the Simons' new house. It was Christmas Eve 1974, and I had left institutionalised care.

# PART III

# 7

# The Four Bs

By the time we arrived in Sittingbourne the sky was pitch black. When the car stopped and everyone got out I was disorientated. It was all totally unfamiliar to me and I had no idea where we were. Everyone helped to carry my few belongings from the car to the house and the walk seemed longer than it really was. It felt very strange, a feeling that is hard to explain. It was an adventure, but at the same time I wondered what was I doing there. I felt as if I were not me, but somebody else. I can't remember any details of that first evening in my new home on Christmas Eve, except bedtime. I had been in my new bed, in my own bedroom, awake, for about two hours. I found it impossible to get off to sleep. My mind was overloaded with thoughts about my new life and Christmas; it was all too much to take in at once and I was very restless. I heard movements and whispers outside my bedroom door. It had been a long time since I had believed in fictitious characters like Father Christmas, and I knew that the sounds coming from outside my door were Betty and Bernard putting out my Christmas presents. When the sounds stopped I waited for a while to make sure they had gone, and then quietly got out of bed to take a quick look outside the bedroom door. Although it was dark I could clearly make out a massive mound of presents. I stared at it in astonishment. I had never seen such a vast array of presents, and they were all mine!

On Christmas morning, I got out of bed early and had a quick check to make sure I hadn't been dreaming. The presents were still outside my room. When I got up and dressed I wished everyone a Happy Christmas. Betty asked me if I had started opening my presents. I said I wasn't sure if I was allowed to. I was told I could, so I attacked the pile immediately. I tore the paper to reveal an inexhaustible supply of games, books and sweets. There were so many presents it took me quite some time to open them all. I'd never had so many new possessions all at once.

The rest of Christmas Day was spent eating and drinking – the drink for me was Coca-Cola and lemonade. The first twenty-four hours in my new home were very memorable but there had been a great deal to take in and by bedtime I was worn out.

It wasn't until the festive season was over that I began to become properly aware of my new surroundings. The new house had been painted fairly recently so it looked very smart. The downstairs of the house consisted of a posh front room, which contained Betty's best furniture; a large hallway; a compact medium-sized kitchen; an indoor lavatory and a small living-room which had patio doors leading out to the garden. Upstairs were a bathroom and toilet, a small landing and airing cupboard and three bedrooms. Betty and Bernard's room was the largest of the three, Billy's bedroom was of medium size and I, Fred, had the small box-room. I liked the new house but couldn't get used to the idea that it was my home. I always thought of it as the Simons' house.

The house was on an estate which went by the name of Manor Grove. It covered a fair amount of land, each house having both a front and a back garden. The Manor Grove Estate was all houses – there were no flats or tower blocks. There was a large play area with swings and a roundabout and a slide surrounded by grass. Some of the roads running round the estate were quite busy but the estate itself was generally quiet with very little traffic. It was a very comfortable place to live, and was well maintained by the council and the tenants.

After the Christmas holidays I started at my new junior school, only a ten-minute walk from Manor Grove. It was called

Barrow Grove, a name I liked; it sounded much friendlier to me than the name of my last school, St Peter's. On my first day, Betty took me to a teacher who looked after me for that day. My first few days at Barrow Grove were bewildering and I felt like an alien. Because I started in January there were no other new children, and I was the only one who didn't know anybody. Everyone but me seemed to know where they were going and what they were supposed to be doing.

Barrow Grove school was well established, although not as old as St Peter's. The building seemed gigantic to me: it was at least six times larger than St Peter's School. I thought I would never find my way around it. Everything – playground, sports fields, canteen, tuck shops – was in the one complex, unlike St Peter's. I liked my new school very much and I worked hard in the lessons. It was a fresh start, and I can honestly say that throughout my short time at Barrow Grove I was never sent out of a classroom. The teachers were very helpful, and I was taught extra reading and writing. Considering that I spent only seven months there before going to senior school I learnt a fair amount. At Barrow Grove I felt content and generally speaking my days there were happy ones.

Not long after starting at Barrow Grove I began to make many new friends, both boys and girls. Some of them weren't even in my class – I would get to know other children in the playground. All the children were very friendly and this helped me to settle down with my new teacher. My new friends didn't make fun of my reading and writing difficulties. Instead they tried to help me. I also made friends on the Manor Grove Estate. The first were two sisters, one of whom was the same age as me and the other a few years younger. We became close very quickly and would often sit around talking or playing games. We got to know some of the boys who lived not far from my house. One of them, Terry, unlike most of the boys on the estate, was a bit stuck up. He was obsessive about checking his shoes for dog shit. When you walked down the road with Terry he would check his shoes for dog shit every few minutes and it became a standing joke.

I had lived in my new home about three or four months before I got talking to the boy who lived opposite me, Clive, who was a couple of years older than me. It was the Easter holidays and as there had been a heavy snowfall in the night we were both outside contemplating what to do. That morning Clive and I mucked about together in the snow.

During the school holidays I would go out with Bernard in the lorry. Because Bernard worked for a scrap metal dealer the cab was very dirty, so whenever I went out in the lorry I would have to wear my old scruffy clothes. Before I was allowed to go, Betty would always tell me to behave myself and do as I was told. Then she would hand me a Tupperware container filled with an assortment of sandwiches, and wish us a good day. On my very first trip out I was amazed by the sheer size of the lorry. It took quite an effort just to climb into the cab. Once inside the cab the first thing that struck you was how messy and dirty it all looked. I didn't remark on this to Bernard, as that might have put an end to the trips in the lorry. The second impression was how high up we were sitting in the lorry cab. Bernard and I hardly ever spoke to one another on these days out – Bernard wasn't what you would call a conversationalist. I spent most of the time looking out of the window. Yet I liked going out with Bernard. The silence was companionable and it gave me a chance to see new places as we drove all around Kent.

When we stopped off at scrap metal yards I stayed in the cab, unless I got out to go to the loo. At some of the yards the men would come up to the cab and have a chat with me, or tell me a joke. I liked this because it made me feel part of things. After a while the men in the yards got to know me and one or two of them used to give me some money for sweets. When this first happened I was astonished. After all, I was only visiting and didn't really know them. I took the money anyway and thanked the yard men. This happened on a few occasions.

One day we were parked in a yard and Bernard had gone off to talk to someone. He was away for a long time and there wasn't anyone else around. Eventually I became bored with waiting and started to poke around in the cab. I wanted to know what was in the large glove compartment. At first I thought I'd better not open it in case Bernard caught me, but as time went on my curiosity got the better of me, so I opened it. Inside there didn't seem to be much of interest, only some rubbish and a filthy pair of gloves. However, when I took a closer look I found a magazine. But it wasn't like any magazine I'd seen before. It was full of pictures of naked women. I could hardly believe my eyes as I turned the dirty, crushed pages. I didn't look through many of the tatty, torn pages of pornography before I quickly put it back in the glove compartment. Bernard would be back any moment, I thought. From that day on I found it impossible to look at Bernard in quite the same light as I had before. I thought that if he ever gave me any hassle I could always threaten to tell Betty about the magazine in his glove compartment. Bernard, however, being Bernard, never did give me any hassle, so I never breathed a word about it to Betty.

As foster parents the Simons had set guidelines by which I was to be brought up. Included in these guidelines was the stipulation that I should undergo regular eye tests and medical examinations, not to mention regular trips to the dentist. Most of them were uneventful, but there was one exception, a check-up at the doctor's. Betty met me from school and took me to the surgery. I had no great liking for doctors, mostly because they made me undress and put freezing cold pieces of metal on me, but the examination seemed to be going all right, and I was in good health. The examination had virtually finished when the doctor handed me what looked like a bit of Betty's Tupperware. I had no idea what was going on. The doctor said to me: 'Can you do a sample in there for me?' I was none the wiser. A sample? What is he on about? I thought.

Betty said: 'He wants you to wee in it.'

I was taken aside and some curtains were drawn around me, and there I was standing in the doctor's surgery with one hand holding my willy and this Tupperware thing in the other.

I had never heard of anything so daft. I think the fact that it seemed so utterly stupid was the reason why I was unable to produce any wee-wee – not so much as a dribble. When I told the doctor this he then ran the tap. This had no effect on me whatsoever. The tap ran for about five minutes before the doctor finally gave up trying to get a sample out of me.

When the examination was over Betty was handed a Tupperware beaker for me to wee in at home. It was now her responsibility to see that my wee-wee got safely to the doctor. On our way to the bus stop, Betty started moaning at me. 'You little bugger! Now I've got to go back to the doctor's with it. You should have gone when the tap was turned on, you little bugger, you!' Luckily, when we arrived at the bus stop a couple of people were already in the queue, which gave me some respite from Betty's nagging. That evening, however, there was a resumption of the lectures about doing a wee-wee at the doctor's. The whole experience had been very strange indeed, but I did have a good laugh to myself when I thought of Betty having to go shopping with my sample in her bag.

Billy spent a lot of time and money improving and upgrading his car. To say that it was his pride and joy would be a gross understatement. It was his first and true love. Sometimes when he went out during the weekend he would take me along for the ride. One Saturday morning I went out with Billy in his car. We went to a garage not far from Sittingbourne, and Billy parked the car on the opposite side of the road, which was a very busy main thoroughfare. He said he would be back in ten minutes, he was just going to talk to a friend of his. I sat waiting, watching the traffic and the goings on to pass the time. The seconds ticked by and still Billy wasn't back. He had been gone much longer than ten minutes. I was now starting to feel the need to go to the toilet. I thought, not to worry, Billy will be back any second now. He must have been gone at least twenty minutes when the urge to go to the toilet became very, very great indeed. Both my hands were on my groin and I was doubled up on the back seat in considerable pain shouting: 'Billy! Billy! I can't wait any longer! Billy!' I stayed in agonising pain on the back seat, shouting for Billy, for another five minutes or so, but there was still no sign of him. Then suddenly it was too late for Billy to do anything, even if he had been there.

I had done my best to hold on, but nature had won the day. I was saturated in urine and so was the back seat of Billy's car. After relieving myself I usually felt better for it, but this time I didn't. I sat there feeling doomed. My clothes clung to me like chewing gum and I was very uncomfortable. The stench of urine only made matters worse. I didn't know what to do, so I just had to sit there and wait for Billy to return. Ten minutes later he finally came back. I don't think he could quite believe his eyes. He opened the driver's door and looked round at me. There was silence. A minute or two later he said, 'What's happened?' It seemed to me that it was quite obvious what had happened, but I explained anyway, adding that it had been an accident. I think Billy was more concerned about his car than about me. Throughout the journey home he didn't speak to me. From where he parked his car you had to walk past at least six houses to get to the Simons' house, and when we reached Manor Grove I felt apprehensive about getting out of the car. I felt so embarrassed – what if anyone saw me? I had wet myself. If the neighbours got to know this I would never live it down. But I had no choice. I got out of the car and walked as quickly as I could to the house. Billy walked fast too, so we both arrived at the front door together. Betty opened the front door, and straight away she knew something had happened, probably by the look on Billy's face, not to mention mine.

Billy told Betty what had happened. She immediately started shouting at me. 'Why didn't you get out of the car? You naughty child! Why did you do it?' I didn't know what to say; after all, I had tried my best to hold on until Billy came back.

'It was an accident,' I said. She whacked me round the head and sent me upstairs to have a bath and change into some clean clothes. When I came downstairs, all nice and clean in a different set of clothes, Billy was bringing in the back seat of his car. Luckily it came out quite easily in two parts, which made the cleaning up job much easier. Betty and Billy set about cleaning the seat in the kitchen. Betty went on at me for the rest of that weekend about wetting myself in Billy's car. She went on and on about how hard he worked on his car, how much he liked his car and how I had done such a terrible thing. The way she went on anyone would have thought I had wet myself deliberately.

Mr and Mrs Simons' official title in the eyes of Dr Barnardo's was that of my foster parents. In theory the Simons were my mum and dad, and Billy was my older brother. However, as with many theories, there comes a flaw when it was put into practice. I didn't call Billy my brother, I simply called him Billy as that was his name. I was perfectly aware that he wasn't my real brother, even if he was my foster brother. Betty and Bernard weren't called Mum and Dad, although they were my foster mum and dad; neither was I to call them Betty and Bernard, although those were their names. No – instead I was instructed by Betty to call them Auntie and Uncle. To me it seemed very odd and silly to call them Auntie Betty and Uncle Bernard, for I knew perfectly well that not only were they not my real mum and dad but they weren't my aunt and uncle either.

As for me, I had long since dropped the 'Al' in Alfred and was always called Fred by my friends and anyone else who knew me well. However, in the Simons' house, I wasn't often called Fred at all, because Betty had taken to calling me Bugger. I would hear her shouting 'You little bugger!' or 'Bugger – come here,' and 'That bugger has been lying again.' And so on and so forth. I became accustomed to being called Bugger, although I knew Betty wasn't using the word affectionately – when I heard 'Bugger' I knew that I was in trouble. I think calling me Bugger made life easier for Betty because it meant we became the four Bs – Betty, Bernard, Billy and Bugger!

# 8
# Close Friends

In 1975 I went on holiday to the Barnardo's camp near Deal once again. That year there were a lot fewer children than before, and no Scouts. I didn't feel part of it all any longer, and somehow I wasn't completely at ease with the other children. I spent most of the time with another boy who was also fostered. I never really felt happy with either the fostered and adopted children or those who lived in care. I had experienced both kinds of life but now I felt I didn't belong in either. The friends I'd made the previous two years weren't there, which only increased my sense of isolation.

Towards the end of the camp we were taken on a day trip to a seaside resort. It was to be the last opportunity to buy things to take back. Although Betty didn't say she wanted me to bring back a present for her or the family I got the distinct impression that if I didn't she would be very cross with me. She certainly didn't tell me not to buy any presents. But by this time I had spent nearly all my money – four pounds and a few pence was all I had left. I thought I should buy something for the Simons with it. I looked around the shops for ages, but saw nothing I wanted to buy. Time was getting on and the shops were starting to close. I hurried into Woolworth's. After browsing around for about five or ten minutes my eyes fell upon a really nice china ornament. I looked at it for a little while before checking the price. No wonder I thought it was nice, it was priced at £35! I was dumbstruck. All that money for one ornament! I had to think of a plan, so I walked around the shop a couple of times mulling ideas over in my head. First I thought I would steal it and hide it under my shirt, but then I realised it was too big. My next idea was just to pick it up off the shelf and run out of the door with it, but it was much too heavy. Then all of a sudden I came up with what I thought was a foolproof plan.

I would find a sticker showing a price I could well afford and swap it with the one on the ornament. This seemed the perfect solution. And so it was that I took the ornament, now priced at a princely 75p up to the cashier. She immediately questioned the ridiculous price, but I said I thought it was right. She then called over the manageress, who went and checked the price. As soon as she came back she started shouting at me: 'You changed the prices, you little thief! Get out of this shop and don't come back again!' I didn't stay around to hear any more. I turned and ran as fast as my legs would carry me. I kept running, running, running until I was too exhausted to run any more. When I regained my breath and felt fully recovered I came to the decision that the Simons weren't getting a holiday present from me. It was all too much bother, and if they asked I would just have to tell them that I had run out of money and was unable to buy them anything.

I looked forward to starting senior school with great anticipation because it made me feel grown up. Many of the kids I knew at Barrow Grove were starting senior school at the same time. It made a big difference, because it meant I would have friends before I even arrived. Most of my new friends on the Manor Grove Estate also attended or were soon to attend Westlands High School. On my first day at Westlands I was dressed in a brand-new uniform, new shoes, with a new school bag and new pens, pencils and ruler. That very first morning, before I left the house for school, Betty made a big fuss about my appearance. I was glad to get out of the door. On the way to Westlands I met up with quite a few of my friends. The walk was a little further than to my old school and quite a bit of the journey was uphill, but because I was with my friends it didn't seem too bad. When I arrived at Westlands High School on my first day the first thing that caught my eye was the teeming masses of children. I had never seen so many, all going to the same place at once. I remembered being in awe of the sheer size of Barrow Grove but it had nothing on Westlands High.

After assembly we were taken to our classroom by our form tutor. The first day we didn't do much school work. Most of the time was taken up with familiarising ourselves with a new system and being shown around the school. By the end of the first week most of the formalities were sorted out and we all roughly knew our way around.

Westlands High School was a large comprehensive in Sittingbourne. Parts of the school were fairly old but there were also a couple of new blocks and many prefabs. The school sports facilities were quite good. There was a massive sports and playing field, although we left the school grounds for cross-country running. There was also a school farm, which was part of the rural science department. The farm grew various crops, and in a separate part they kept a few animals: a couple of pigs, a goat and some chickens.

Once I got used to my new school and settled down, I began to take an interest in my school work. I always tried my best. I wanted to do well and enjoyed the work and I was also desperate to impress the Simons. I thought that if I got a good school report, Betty would be happy and pleased with me. I liked going to Westlands very much; I liked the lessons, the school and the teachers. I never dreaded going to school; in fact I looked forward to it. I was never sent out of a class or kept in detention, although I daresay I was probably told off a couple of times. I have only happy memories of Westlands High.

My circle of friends was growing even larger. To add to those I had on the estate and from Barrow Grove, I also made new friends at Westlands, children in my form and some from other classes, and I was never short of company. Sometimes I felt some of them were more intelligent than me, but this didn't pose any problems. None of them ever suggested that I was less able than them at school work. Much has happened since those days, and it is many years since I last saw any of them – I can't even remember some of their names – but I have always been grateful to have known such friendly and caring people.

On the way to school the estate children met up by calling round for one another, and we would talk all the way there. Although I wasn't in the same class as any of them, I would always walk to and from school with them. One day we were all talking about sports and it became clear that not only did we all enjoy sports and games but we all had some sort of sports equipment or game at home. I had a bar-football game, the boy who was next on the way to school had a table tennis table in his garage, the third boy had a dartboard in his bedroom and the boy who lived nearest the school had a full-sized snooker table in his living-room.

So every Tuesday or Wednesday night we would all converge on someone's house and have a games night – we generally organised some sort of competition amongst ourselves, and more often than not the person whose house it was won the competition. Other than bar-football I wasn't exactly outstanding at any of the games: I enjoyed taking part but I rarely did very well in the competitions. Most of all I loved playing table tennis and snooker. The games nights were a great success; not only were they fun but we all got to know one another quite well and this strengthened our friendships.

It wasn't long after I got to know Alison and Joanne, the two sisters on the Manor Grove Estate, that we started seeing a lot of each other. I cannot remember whose idea it was – probably Alison's – but we decided that we wanted to go to the Saturday morning pictures. Neither the sisters' parents nor Betty objected – in fact, they gladly gave us the money to go. They were probably pleased to see us doing something constructive rather than hanging around the estate all morning. Until then, I had rarely been to the pictures. The cinema was in Sittingbourne town centre and we always walked there. It cost about 25p or 30p to get in and for that we got to see some cartoons, a mini-film and part of a serial. The cartoons and the mini-film were quite good, but the serials were irritating because they would come on last, and there would always be a cliffhanger at the end so that you had to return the following week to find out what happened next. For me the pictures were the highlight of the week.

Next we started going swimming on Saturday afternoons. Before moving to Sittingbourne I hadn't grasped the basic technique of swimming; in fact I swam like a brick. At school in PE the class was often taken to Sittingbourne baths. There I was given lessons with a few others who were unable to swim. I hadn't got the hang of it, but I wasn't afraid of the water and enjoyed trying. After several Saturday afternoons at the baths with Alison and Joanne I soon began to improve. Once I learned to swim properly we had even more fun on a Saturday afternoon. The sisters played a vital part in helping me to learn to swim, providing much-needed encouragement. I felt great when I managed to swim my first length of the pool, and they were so pleased for me.

Saturdays were then a very special day for me. In the morning there were the pictures and in the afternoon we would go swimming. I had never been so active, and my life was full and happy.

Before moving to Sittingbourne I had never even sat on a push-bike, let alone ridden one. There I was, eleven years old, and unable to ride a bike. I had never owned a bike nor had access to one. The majority of my friends on the Manor Grove Estate had their own bikes and all of them could cycle pretty well. On days when they got their bikes out and cycled up and down the paths and pavements I would just sit and watch. They soon saw that I was feeling a bit left out so they suggested I borrow their bikes and we could all take it in turns to ride. I had to admit then that I didn't know how to ride a bike. They immediately set to work teaching me how. After many hours, days and quite a few accidents I began to grasp the basics of cycling. Then one day I suddenly found myself cycling down the path on my own. My friends were standing at the opposite end and as I approached them, cycling with no assistance, they began to clap and cheer. I had done it, I could ride a bike!

Betty owned a small green push-bike which she used occasionally when going to visit her mother. The bike was fairly old and had very small wheels, but it was reliable. Now that I could ride a bike (just about), I approached Betty about the possibility of borrowing her bike now and again. At first, she was less than enthusiastic, but eventually she agreed, on the condition that I paid for any damage I caused and that I didn't ride on the roads. So now I could cycle around happily with my friends, and I began to feel that I was a part of things.

One day, Alison, Clive (the boy who lived opposite me) and I came up with the idea of forming a small select gang. To have a gang you needed a gang meeting-place. We gave the matter a lot of thought. In the end we came to the conclusion that Clive's shed was ideal for the purpose. Clive wasn't too sure about it but agreed to ask his mother if we could use it for our gang hut. Clive's mother was fairly easy-going and she said we could use it as long as we didn't make too much noise.

First we tidied up the small garden shed. It wasn't long before we had it in order and seats in place for the members. The gang then had to have a name. I've forgotten it now, but in any case it changed about as often as the weather. As well as a gang name we had a secret knock and password. One or both were (sometimes) needed to get into the gang hut. The membership of our gang consisted only of Clive, Alison and myself. Not long after we had got things started Joanne wanted to join, and after much deliberation in a gang meeting we decided she could. In total there were just the four of us, but we didn't want any more members as there wasn't much room in the gang hut. I can't remember the gang getting up to much but it was good to have our own exclusive society and a private little meeting-place. It gave me a sense of belonging that I had never had before.

A few weeks after the gang hut had been established Alison decided that we needed some stationery. Why, I don't know. Writing letters and keeping files was hardly our thing. She told me that the gang stationery could be obtained from Woolworth's without too much difficulty. This, of course, meant without paying. I didn't think about the matter seriously: after all, it was only a few bits of paper and stuff. I hadn't stolen anything for a long time, not since I left Tunbridge Wells, so I was quite out of practice. In a way I felt compelled to do it. Alison was willing to steal, and I would have felt rather silly refusing. The fact that it was for the gang gave the whole expedition to

Woolworth's an even greater sense of purpose. After the plans had been finalised the following Saturday the two of us went into Sittingbourne town centre and made our way to Woolworth's. We pulled off the stationery job with some ease. The rest of the afternoon we spent playing with the stolen stationery, congratulating each other on how well we had handled the robbery. We weren't exactly Bonnie and Clyde, but at least we weren't caught.

The very same weekend, on Saturday night, Betty stormed into my little bedroom looking very angry indeed. I had no idea what had upset her so, but it wasn't long before I found out.

'What is this?' she demanded, holding in her hand a brand-new rubber.

I thought to myself, 'Stupid old woman, if you don't know what it is now, you'll never know.' At length I answered, 'It's a rubber.'

'I know that, you little bugger,' Betty retorted in a loud roar, 'but what is it doing in your pocket?'

After a minute or two's silence I replied: 'I don't know.'

Betty was full of rage. She slapped me around the head. 'Don't tell me such lies. Where did you get this?'

Again there was a brief silence. 'I found it.' The rubber was brand new and clearly it didn't look like it had been found on the ground or anything. Somehow Betty knew I had stolen it right from the beginning of the conversation but I'd only said I'd found it because I didn't want to upset her.

'It's stolen, isn't it? You little bugger, you!'

I could tell by the look on her face that she was well wound up. I wondered why, if she knew what it was doing in my pocket and that I had stolen it, she was asking me these silly questions. But she wasn't after information. She wanted me to admit I had stolen it and eventually I did, after a lot of interrogation and after being called an ungrateful little bugger several times. However, I never did tell the full story because I didn't want my friends to get into trouble. That particular night I wanted to go out with them to the fair, but my punishment for stealing was that I had to stay in that night and all the following week.

# 9

# My Best Isn't Good Enough

Among the enormous load of presents I got at Christmas 1975 was a fishing rod, a reel and some tackle. I had never been fishing before I lived with the Simons, and when I saw Bernard and Billy setting off I always wanted to go as well. It wasn't that fishing held any great attraction for me but rather that I didn't like being left out of any of the family's leisure activities. Once I had been equipped, I was included in the fishing expeditions, but we weren't long into my first fishing trip before I came to the conclusion that it was boring and a waste of time. Given a choice I would have preferred to mess about on the estate with my friends. However, when a fishing trip was mentioned I would try to pretend to be enthusiastic – after all, they had spent quite a bit of money on my fishing stuff and I didn't want the Simons to think I was ungrateful.

If fishing didn't capture my imagination, I loved being outdoors. Bernard's parents owned a fruit farm not far from Sittingbourne. It was huge, stretching for acres, apparently without boundaries, like the woods at St Christopher's had seemed when I was younger. Billy owned an air rifle which he used on his grandparents' farm. He didn't shoot at anything live, only at a printed target. One day he took me shooting. I had never seen a gun in action, let alone used one before. Under Billy's supervision I had a go. I didn't know about the kick-back on guns so when I fired my first shot the gun-sights hit me in the eye. I escaped without a black eye and learnt one thing: that I had no great skills at shooting.

When I moved to Sittingbourne, Jim Johnson remained my social worker. I got on reasonably well with Jim. I knew him from the Barnardo's camps and knew he was a decent sort. I never knew when he was going to turn up until he arrived in his red Renault car. Betty only ever told me he was coming if I wanted to go off somewhere when she was expecting him. During these visits Jim would ask me about my well-being and about my home life with the Simons. I always told him that life was OK and that I was getting on all right. He would ask if there were any problems. I never thought there were: I always tried my best not to please myself but to please the Simons, or rather Betty – Bernard and Billy were not very demanding. Often when Jim came I would be out playing with friends, and on those days the conversation didn't last long. I was always itching to get back to whatever we'd been doing.

And yet I never felt that Betty liked me. She never seemed at all pleased with me, and no matter how hard I tried I cannot remember her praising me for anything. I felt that when I was in her house I was in the way and was nothing but a nuisance. Betty didn't treat me as her younger son, but more like a naughty stray dog that had come into her house and shit on the carpet. She expected me to be very, very grateful to them all the time for being my foster parents. I was grateful, of course, for what they did for me, but I felt she was overlooking the important point that they had taken me on for their sakes as well as mine. I didn't go to them and ask to be fostered – they came to Barnardo's to get a 'brother' for Billy. As for Bernard's attitude towards me – well there wasn't one, really, because he never said much at all, nor did he ever punish me. He just went along with his wife, and whatever she said or did he never objected to, at least not in front of me. Billy was, on the surface, quite friendly, but I don't think he was totally happy with the idea of a younger brother. He seemed very keen to show me in a bad light to Betty. For instance, if I accidentally broke something in the house, he would take great delight in running off to tell her what I had done. I didn't dislike Billy, but I never looked upon him as my brother, and although I enjoyed his company sometimes, he was always too much of a mummy's boy for us to have a really good laugh.

Calm was not a word you would associate with Betty. She had little patience and a very short fuse. Instead of talking to me quietly she would more often than not shout at me. It wasn't always because I had done something wrong; it was merely Betty's customary method of communicating with me. I began to resent Betty shouting at me all day for what seemed such trivial things; washing my hands, perhaps, or combing my hair. I found one way to get my own back on Betty, although I was quite intimidated by her, and that was to pretend I didn't hear her. That really got her going. Sometimes her wrath would spill over and not only would she shout but she resorted to hitting me. The slaps seemed to come from nowhere, around the back of the head, or a whack on the legs and a clip around the ear. By this time I had come to the conclusion that this was the way all adults acted in their own homes and that was that. It wasn't so much that I expected that sort of behaviour from adults, but I was certainly always prepared for it.

One day I was having a nice warm bath. Betty was shouting her head off up the stairs. 'Hurry up out of the bath! People want to get in there!' At that moment I realised that no one would come in while I was still bathing or in the bathroom. So, from that day onwards, I used the bathroom as a sanctuary. It meant I could spend less time in the presence of the Simons when I was in their house. Most of the time I was at school, or outside playing. I was indoors only at mealtimes, bathtime, bedtime and when it rained. I liked the peace of the bathroom so much that I'd often stay an hour. This didn't go down too well with the Simons, but I clung obstinately to my Betty-free zone. Eventually my elongated bathtimes became legendary in the Simons' household. Betty was often to be found saying, 'I don't know what he does in there all that time.' I casually whiled away the minutes just lolling around, relaxing in the warm water. I couldn't help but hear Betty's repetitive and impotent shouts booming through the bathroom door, but I was out of harm's way and she couldn't touch me.

KENT COUNTY COUNCIL EDUCATION DEPARTMENT

**WESTLANDS HIGH SCHOOL SITTINGBOURNE**

NAME ALFRED FEVER FORM 1B1

REPORT FOR HALF YEAR ENDING 19th FEBRUARY 1976

No. of half-day absences 0 No. of detentions

Position of responsibility —

| Subject | Term | Exam | Teachers' Comments |
|---|---|---|---|
| ENGLISH | C+ | | Alfred tries hard and produces some good work. |
| MATHEMATICS | C+ | | Alfred tries very hard and has achieved some pleasing results |
| GEOGRAPHY | C | | Alfred tries hard |
| RELIGIOUS EDUCATION | C- | | Alfred tries very hard |
| ~~FRENCH~~ READING | B- | | Alfred tries hard |
| HISTORY | C+ | | Alfred's work is satisfactory |
| BIOLOGY | C | | Alfreds work is satisfactory. He will work hard. He has a pleasant, extrovert character which enables him to communicate well orally. |
| CHEMISTRY | | | |
| PHYSICS | | | |
| INTEGRATED SCIENCE | C | | Alfred tries hard. His work has improved lately |
| RURAL SCIENCE | C+ | | Alfred tries very hard. Shows an interest |
| | | | |
| MUSIC | C | | Some good work |
| DRAMA | C | | Has made a good start in drama, lacks confidence |
| ART/DESIGN | C+ | | Alfred always works well |
| DOMESTIC SCIENCE | | | |
| NEEDLEWORK | | | |
| METALWORK | | | |
| WOODWORK | | | |
| TECHNICAL DRAWING | | | |
| | | | |
| PHYSICAL EDUCATION | C+ | | Quite good |

GRADES: A = Very Good B = Good C= Average D = Below Average E = Unsatisfactory

Form Teacher's Comments Fred tries hard and is a helpful member of the form. He needs to overcome his fear of being behind the other children in the class with his work

Signature B. Newman

Head of Lower/~~Middle~~ School's Comments A very pleasant personality and I am pleased to see that he is working so well.

Signature L J Rositer

b.a. Jemett Signature of Headmaster

000815B

KENT COUNTY COUNCIL EDUCATION DEPARTMENT

**WESTLANDS HIGH SCHOOL SITTINGBOURNE**

NAME ALFRED FEVER FORM 1B1

REPORT FOR HALF YEAR ENDING 21st JULY 1976

No. of half-day absences 0 No. of detentions

Position of responsibility FORM CAPTAIN

| Subject | Term | Exam | Teachers' Comments |
|---|---|---|---|
| ENGLISH | B | 74% | Fred tries very hard and obtains satisfactory results |
| MATHEMATICS | C+ | 54% | Fred perseveres with his maths, but sometimes has difficultie[s] |
| GEOGRAPHY | C+ | 47½ | Fred tries hard and works enthusiasticall[y] |
| RELIGIOUS EDUCATION | C+ | 73 | Fred has gained confidence and done well |
| ~~FRENCH~~ READING | B | | Fred has made excellent progress |
| HISTORY | B– | 62% | Fred has made very good progress |
| BIOLOGY | B– | B+ | A good enthusiastic worker who is making excellent progress. Well done Fred. |
| CHEMISTRY | | | |
| PHYSICS | | | |
| INTEGRATED SCIENCE | C | 54% | Fred takes an interest in his work |
| RURAL SCIENCE | C+ | 20/30 | Tries hard and is gaining confidence |
| | | | |
| MUSIC | C+ | | Fred always tries hard |
| DRAMA | C+ | 34% | Fred has worked hard all year, well done |
| ART/DESIGN | C+ | | Always works well |
| DOMESTIC SCIENCE | | | |
| NEEDLEWORK | | | |
| METALWORK | | | |
| WOODWORK | | | |
| TECHNICAL DRAWING | | | |
| | | | |
| PHYSICAL EDUCATION | C | | Good effort made |

GRADES: A = Very Good B = Good C= Average D = Below Average E = Unsatisfactory

Form Teacher's Comments Fred is a pleasant helpful boy. He has made good progress and this should continue if he tries hard. He is also outgrowing his immaturity.

Signature E Newman

Head of Lower/~~Middle~~ School's Comments Fred is really keen to give satisfaction in his work and anxious to learn.

Signature L J Rossiter

b a Jerrett Signature of Headmaster

0008158

Pages 97 and 98 show my school reports from Westlands High School. The effort I put into my school work is clearly evident from the teachers' comments.

Throughout the time I lived in Sittingbourne I had no contact with my natural parents whatsoever. My social worker informed my parents that I had been fostered. While they weren't exactly overjoyed about it, they were in no position to offer me a better alternative so they had no real grounds for objection. When my social worker suggested to the Simons that my parents might be interested in making contact with me, the Simons weren't keen on the idea. In fact they were dead against it. My social worker, meeting with such definite resistance, didn't pursue the matter further. This kept Betty content. I had now reached the age of twelve and had never seen my real parents, nor did I know anything about them.

One day Jim came to see me for a chat. What he had to say was very peculiar. This year, he said, I would be going on two holidays, rather than one. My first holiday would be at somewhere called Highbroom and then I would go on to the Barnardo's camp. This seemed rather unusual but I had no objection to two holidays. I knew the little village of Highbroom just down the road from Tunbridge Wells. I thought it sounded all right. I would be able to go and visit my old friends in Tunbridge Wells, I thought.

I was in good spirits when Jim came to collect me for my first holiday, but during the journey I became uneasy. As we neared our destination it became clear that I had made a mistake; we were nowhere near the Highbroom I knew. Eventually we arrived at a huge, forbidding mansion – the type of house that looms up at the start of a horror film. The only thing missing was the eerie background music signifying impending doom.

Highbroom – this Highbroom, anyway – was not a Kentish village but a children's home. In fact it was seven miles from Tunbridge Wells, near Crowborough in East Sussex. I didn't like the look of the place from the start. It was stuck out in the middle of nowhere, and any hopes of seeing my old friends went out of the window. My one-week stay at Highbroom wasn't a happy one. I didn't take to the place or the staff, or even many of the children, but I kept on saying to myself, don't worry, it's only for a week; only a couple more days now and I will be out of this place for good. The knowledge that I wouldn't be there the following week was what kept me going in this depressing institution where I had landed out of the blue. Sure enough, the wretched week came to an end and I was looking forward to Barnardo's summer camp with more enthusiasm than usual. After my horrible experience at Highbroom I was relieved to get out of the Hammer Horror house. I'd hated my stay there and I never wanted to see the place again.

The Barnardo's camp was different this time: instead of tents at Deal we stayed just outside Folkestone in a disused converted school. The amenities and the general condition of the place were far superior to what we had had at previous camps. Again the numbers were reduced, but this year I had a really good time. Part of the reason I was much happier was that I met up with a few of my old friends. The two brothers I'd met the first year were there, and I was overjoyed to see that John was, too. It was great to see them all again and chat about times gone by and to make plans for what we might get up to on the holiday. In contrast to the year before I didn't feel out of place, quite the reverse. I was completely at ease with my old friends. I suppose they were just about the only constants in my disjointed life, and I really felt I belonged with them. A lot of time had passed since I had last seen them, but they hadn't changed much and it wasn't long before we were having a good laugh. The two-week holiday went quickly, helped along by the usual antics, laughs, silliness and fun.

On the second to last day of the camp my social worker, Jim Johnson, who was running the camp, asked to speak to me. I went with him and sat in his car, wondering what I had done wrong. I couldn't think of any other reason why he should want to talk to me alone in the car. I had only been there a minute when he dropped a bombshell on me that blew up my whole world. He said: 'Fred, you won't be going back to your foster parents after this holiday. You're going to Highbroom.'

I was totally shocked by this devastating news, I just couldn't speak.

'Mrs Simons says she can't cope and is ill, so you have to go back into a children's home,' Jim went on.

I thought, this isn't real, it's not happening, surely this is a mistake. I am not going back to a children's home . . .

'I didn't tell you at the beginning of the camp because it would only have meant that you wouldn't have enjoyed your holiday.'

It wasn't a nightmare, it really *was* happening. I couldn't take it all in properly, nor could I think clearly of the full implications. Still in deep shock, I thought of Highbroom for the first time since I'd gratefully left its gates and the ghastly week I'd spent there. Now they were going to send me there for good.

My mind went back to the early years spent at St Christopher's with Jenny and Peter. In my shock and bewilderment I forgot the awful years of abuse that went on afterwards at Tunbridge Wells and, clinging on to what I knew, to a half-remembered time of happiness, I said, 'If I have got to go back to a children's home I want to go back to Tunbridge Wells.' The last day of the camp passed like a waking nightmare, and before the situation had properly sunk in everyone had gone and I was left on my own with my social worker. As we drove along he explained that I couldn't go back to St Christopher's because it was full. Thereafter little conversation passed between us. My feelings or aspirations obviously weren't of any importance. All too soon we were back at the entrance of Highbroom.

# PART IV

# 10
# Welcome Home

As my social worker drove in through the main entrance of Highbroom my heart sank. I felt extremely tense; overwhelmed by it all. It was as if I had been taken from the dock and was being led away to the prison without any memory of the offence or the trial. The car went slowly up the long driveway, avoiding the large potholes, and the awfulness of Highbroom came upon me like a bolt from a crossbow. I wanted to shout and scream and make an almighty protest, but I was still too shocked to utter a word. Inside I felt that there would be no getting out of this, I had been shipped here and that was that. Why, why, why? I just had no answer.

We went in through the enormous main door and my social worker went off for a minute or two. He returned with the head of the home, Mr Jenton. After a brief chat my social worker departed, and I was shown to the playroom. I sat alone feeling ill; nobody seemed keen to speak to me nor I to them. I just could not adjust to these circumstances, it was simply too much to bear. Obviously Highbroom was where rejects were sent, and I was a reject. As the sun shone on that summer's day, I felt cold and miserable. I wanted to go home – but where was home? I had no home. Unwanted, unloved and unable to understand what was going on I sat alone for I don't know how long until it was lunchtime. I felt compelled to eat, to save getting into trouble, but I really had no desire for food, no desire for drink and no desire for living. The rest of the day passed much as before, relieved only by the odd sentence of conversation with a couple of the other children. Bedtime came and went and made me feel worse. I stayed awake all night but I was still no nearer understanding what had happened.

In the short space of time it took to bump up the drive of Highbroom I think a major transformation took place within me. Until then I had had respect for most adults and authority. That isn't to say I respected all adults: in some cases, I held little regard for them. During my transformation all this was to change – that respect was now a thing of the past. On entering Highbroom I looked upon adults and authority as the vile enemy. I had been utterly betrayed. I felt nothing but anger and contempt for the people that I was supposed to look up to. Adults, I'd been led to believe when I was younger, were people to be emulated. But adults were untrustworthy, unreliable and undesirable people and I wanted nothing to do with any of them. Their words were meaningless. The 'us and them' had been triggered off. The fight had now begun.

Highbroom, built before the 1900s, was dark, cold and institutional, a world away from the modern, family-house atmosphere of Domaris. The main entrance hallway was huge, with a wooden stairway at one side. The floor was polished wood. The fireplace might have relieved the gloom had anyone ever lit a fire in it. One of the doors from the hallway led into the cavernous dining-room, where several tables, each seating five or six people, stood on the uncarpeted floor. Children's voices echoed round the room and heels clacked on the bare wood, and it always seemed dark, even in the summer or when the lights were on. Nothing brightened up the dreary room. Another smaller room, where the senior children watched television and ate their meals, led off from the main hall. They had a small adjacent kitchen where they cooked their own breakfast. Next door was an immense room which we younger children used as a television room. The fireplace and an enormous bookshelf dwarfed the television.

Opposite the television room and down a passageway was a small cubicle like a public lavatory, where the children's phone could be found. The walls were painted white but littered with phone numbers and scrawls. Across the passage from the phone was the washroom and laundry room, which had a large roomy airing cupboard. A couple of steps away from the washroom was the kitchen, again vast, but filled with outsize furniture so that it resembled a giant's kitchen. A massive table took up most of the space, and the cooker alone was six feet by four. There were voluminous unfamiliar-looking pots and pans, scarred with years of use. It smelled of disinfectant and yesterday's cooking. Next door was a scullery where vegetables were prepared and the washing-up was done. The old walk-in larder had ageing mouse traps on the floor. At the end of a dingy passageway was the 'playroom'. The high ceiling and huge bay windows at least made the playroom light, but its shabby and outdated furniture was depressing and institutional. Next to the playroom was a large office, a staff room and an office combined, really. The office, which was primarily used by Mr Jenton, had a couple of desks, a filing cabinet and a large cupboard. This part of the building also housed the boys' toilet and an area where the shoes and boots were kept. The conservatory also served a couple of other purposes, with lockers and a cloakroom.

The upstairs of Highbroom was a warren of gloomy passages. Some parts of the upstairs – where the girls slept and Mr and Mrs Jenton's living quarters were – I never even saw. There were many different levels and many corridors, bathrooms, toilets, large bedrooms and a few dormitories. These slept five or six to a room, the large bedrooms took three or four, the small rooms slept two to a room and I think there were a couple of single rooms. Each child had a bed, a small bedside cabinet and one chest of drawers shared between two.

Highbroom was set in many acres of land, a fair amount of which was unspoiled by humans. One of the acres Mr Jenton put to use for growing various vegetable crops. In front of the house was a very large front lawn, and to the side of the house there was another lawn which was split in two, one side used for tennis, the other for volleyball. No more than a couple of yards from the vegetable crops was a makeshift football pitch. The rest of the grounds were generally left uncultivated. In the grounds there was a dangerous old pulley and even an outdoor swimming pool. The swimming pool wasn't maintained and was generally filled with leaves and debris. It was cleaned out only twice while I lived at Highbroom, and I swam in it on one of those occasions. I wasn't keen from the start but the other children talked me into it. It was shallow even in the deep end, and the water felt like ice. The temperature of the water put me off ever swimming in it again. There was also a large hut, one half of which was used as a garage, the other as a play hut for the children. There were also a few other buildings not far from the main house, one of which was a small cottage.

Mr Jenton and his wife were not a young couple. They were probably in their fifties and looked every day of it. Mr Jenton stood about five feet ten inches tall. He was overweight and a large stomach preceded him wherever he went. He had a dark complexion and wore his hair in a brushed-back style, kept in place with the aid of half a ton of Brylcreem. His clothes were drab and his personality matched them: he didn't speak to us children unless it was necessary and when he did speak it was usually in a short, snappy sentence. He might stretch the sentence a bit and raise his voice if he was telling us off. Mrs Jenton was a formidable woman, tall and heavily built. She had grey, curly hair, an enormous bust and colossal muscular arms. Her wrinkled face had a yellowish tinge. She looked – and was – an awesome woman who was capable of putting fear into man and beast, and she did so on many occasions. With her broad Scottish accent sometimes she spoke clearly and abruptly, but other times she would mumble and be quite incoherent. She loved to shout. I think it was one of her hobbies. When she did shout you knew all about it. Even Betty would have been no match for her.

There was no question about who ruled the household: clearly it was Mrs Jenton. Second in command were the Edmonds. The Edmonds lived at the end of the drive in a small house called the Lodge with their son and daughter. Both probably in their early forties, they came from Wales, although neither of them had a particularly strong accent. Mr Edmonds was chubby with curly black hair, fairly tall and quite muscular. Often he would be in a chirpy, happy mood, singing rhymes and silly verses, and as soon as a sunny day broke out he would be in his shorts and summer shirt. Mrs Edmonds was a quiet, bespectacled woman with close-cropped hair. Her clothes, attitudes, opinions and general outlook on life were very conservative, and both Mr and Mrs Edmonds held strong religious convictions.

Two other staff who lived in were a young couple, Simon and Melanie, who later married. Simon stood about six feet six inches tall, was quite thin and spidery, and wore glasses with bottle-bottom lenses. He had a bony face and receding dark brown hair. Simon would be perfectly all right one minute and then fly into an uncontrollable rage the next; his rages were sporadic and unpredictable. He was a religious fanatic. He wore Jesus sandals and a crucifix, and had a guitar which was plastered with religious stickers. Melanie, who shared his religious fervour, was quite a short woman, about five foot two, and fairly plain-looking. She wasn't forceful herself but whatever went on got back to Simon immediately. She played only a very minor role in my life at Highbroom.

There were others who came in during the day and evenings, some part of the staff team, others cooks and cleaners. After I had been living at Highbroom for some time new members of staff came to the home, one of whom was Jackie, a sweet-faced woman in her early twenties. She was fairly caring and intelligent. She lived a long way from Crowborough and would go home for holidays and weekends to Surrey, where her family and boyfriend lived.

On average at any one time there were thirty children at Highbroom, and many of them had brothers and sisters with them in the home. Long before I arrived there had once been eight members of the same family living there. Including myself there was a total of seven boys and two girls who didn't have any brothers and sisters at Highbroom. Some of the families were complete (with the exception of their parents), while others had other brothers and sisters who lived with their natural parents. When I moved into Highbroom there were only six girls among the thirty children.

My first week at Highbroom went very slowly. Time dragged day and night, every hour seemed like a day and every day like a week. I found life very daunting and difficult, and the feeling of isolation did not diminish with the passing of time. It was still the school holidays, and I should have been filling my days with my friends in Sittingbourne. Instead all I could do was sit and think how badly my life had now turned out. I had a roof over my head but I felt homeless. I still had no idea why I was in a children's home. I learnt my way around the necessary parts of the colossal house and explored some of the grounds, deep in thought.

My social worker turned up unexpectedly halfway through the week with my belongings. I came downstairs, surprised to see Jim Johnson unloading from his car into the hallway all my things from Sittingbourne. I looked coldly at the stacks of toys, books and clothes. Some of the other children came into the hall to have a look at what was going on. Some of them stared in awe at the sight of so many toys and games. As they chattered excitedly about the new boy's toys I looked intensely at my things and thought that I would like to make a bonfire out of the whole damned lot. My material possessions meant nothing to me, they served only as a nasty-tasting reminder of the life that was now over. I didn't want those toys. I wanted a proper mum and dad.

Crowborough is a small town in East Sussex. In those days there were very few shops and the shops that did exist sold little of interest. Yet the town did provide a focal point for children and adults alike. Being a rural place there was a very poor bus service. Not that there was much of a high life to travel to – no cinema or other entertainment, just pubs. The population was generally made up of middle- and upper-class people. Most of the surrounding areas consisted of farms and farmland, most of which could be reached only by very narrow and winding roads.

Within two or three weeks of moving to Crowborough I

St Christopher's nursery (1965).
Me sucking my thumb
(*first left, front row*).

In the living-room
playing with my toys,
aged two-and-a-half.

'Just like that!'

Me and my very first girlfriend.

1968: Jenny and Peter's wedding, a wedding with a difference! (*I'm in the middle next to the page-boy*.)

Busy making mischief with my best friends.

A Royal visit. I look up, bemused, at Princess Margaret.

A 'family outing'.

My first day at school.

On holiday at
Greatstone, of which
I have fondest
memories.

Being cheeky, but this
is the nearest I have
ever got to owning a car.

The famous Buster Bill suit.

Saying 'cheese' for the school photographer.

I was always keen to make a fuss of animals.

Me with Pauline Baker on her prize-giving day.

received a couple of letters. They were from my friends in Sittingbourne. One was from Alison and Joanne on the Manor Grove Estate. They also sent a present, some sweets. I was shocked that my friends now knew I had been taken back into care. I felt extremely embarrassed. I didn't want them to know that I was in a children's home. I didn't reply to their letter, although I wanted to say thank you. There was no way I could face writing to Sittingbourne now that that once happy life was over. Until the letters arrived I had been blocking out Sittingbourne from my thoughts. Crowborough and Sittingbourne could not co-exist in my mind – there just wasn't the room. Highbroom in itself was ghastly but when set against Sittingbourne it grew more monstrous still.

The other letter was from a school friend. A self-addressed envelope was enclosed. On the face of it I had no reason not to reply, but again, I couldn't face it. I just felt too ashamed to write. I felt like a prisoner, taken from my home, taken from the community and put away in a gruesome jail, allowed to communicate only by letter. I would've had to have written a pack of lies had I replied; after all I could hardly write 'Having a great time, wish you were here!' and meant it. The letters signified two things to me: they were a painful reminder of a better life and they showed that I had true and loyal friends who cared about me. Unfortunately they lived in Sittingbourne. The fact that I didn't reply made me feel guilty but I told myself it was for the best.

The new school where I started only a week or so after arriving at Highbroom was called Beacon Comprehensive. Beacon School was very large, with over 1,000 pupils, because it served a very wide area encompassing many of the small villages and farms. I didn't want to start another new school and I didn't want to go to school in Crowborough. I had done well at Westlands, and had I gone back there for the second year I would have been moved up a class; I had been told that before breaking up for the summer holidays. I had been pleased that my hard work had been rewarded. At the beginning of my summer holidays I had looked forward to starting back at

Westlands in the new higher class. The thought of starting at yet another school literally made me feel ill. As if it wasn't bad enough moving to a new area, and being put back into care like some piece of electrical goods being taken back to the shop while still under warranty for being faulty.

As soon as I got to the school teachers started passing judgement on me and labelling me as a Dr Barnardo's child. The in-care factor put me in a special category straight away – many children in care were, and still are, discriminated against in this way. Not long after the basic formalities were over, the teacher got me to do an IQ test. Before I even put pen to paper I knew where my destiny lay; the bottom class. Lo and behold I was correct. The bastards had done it! I was exiled to the bottom class yet again. The bastards! Although I knew it was going to happen long before it did, deep down I nursed a small hope that somehow I wouldn't have to suffer that dreadful fate. Putting me into the bottom class was the last act of their despicable play. They could do no more damage to me now, they had taken my home from me, they had taken my friends from me and now, finally, they had taken my chance for an education from me. From the moment I started at Beacon School I realised that it wasn't a place where my education would flourish. I had been taken away from the school in which I would have flourished.

After being placed in the bottom class I could see no point in trying hard at school. Once you were put in the bottom class you knew there was no way out, and that no matter how hard you worked you would always be there. Because of this I adopted an attitude that it didn't really matter what I did, because the teachers would always see me as unintelligent. Yet I did still try at school until my second year, but after that I gave up. My life was so horrible that I really didn't give a shit about anything. I hated authoritarian people, and during my short life I had had a great deal of contact with such people. I saw teachers as oppressive adults who were part of the system, and who were in collusion with Barnardo's. I hated the teachers at Beacon School, but I hated Barnardo's staff even more. The teachers, although strict, didn't have the power to punish me like the staff at Barnardo's did, so their ability to frighten me was much reduced. Unlike other children in the class, I was very familiar with constant confrontation with authoritarian adults. As time went on I had more and more problems outside school, and so my behaviour and school work deteriorated to the extent that there was little or no point in me even attending.

For some children doing well at school meant that they would one day get a decent job. I knew that even if I'd tried and had done well at school there would be no way I would get a decent job. After all, what use were CSEs when other children were taking O-Levels from the beginning? I realised that it was all a waste of time. The carrot and the stick didn't work for me. I was used to the stick and the carrot wasn't worth having.

To match its institutional atmosphere Highbroom had many rules and regulations which dictated my life from the time I got up until the time I went to bed. A rule to say what time to get up, a rule to say what time to be downstairs after bed-making. A rule about saying grace, a rule about what you could eat and how much you could eat. We had to get back from school by a fixed time and change out of our school uniform as soon as we got in. Before teatime we had to show our clean and shiny shoes to a member of staff. If the shoes didn't come up to the mark we would have to go away and clean them until they met with approval. There was a rule about washing your hands before a meal, a set day and time for having a bath and hair wash, a set time for going to bed.

No drinking alcohol, no smoking, no chewing gum, no swearing, no earring-wearing if you were a boy. Doing exactly as you were told by a member of staff.

As well as all those rules and regulations, there were fixed forms of address for the staff. Mr and Mrs Jenton and Mr and Mrs Edmonds were called exactly that but the other members of staff, like Simon, Melanie and Jackie, had to be addressed as Uncle Simon, Auntie Melanie, and so on. I really did object to these unfamiliar and sometimes horrid people being accorded the right to pose as my family. This blatant misuse of the words 'auntie' and 'uncle' was to me and many other children an insult.

Dr Barnardo's roots as an organisation are strongly religious, and this emphasis on religion came to the fore on Sundays. On Sundays we weren't allowed to wear our usual clothes in the morning. We had to dress in our Sunday best. The term Sunday best was hardly apt: the clothes weren't at all stylish, the ones we ourselves preferred; they were the clothes the staff decided we would wear. For the boys Sunday best meant a naff-looking jacket; for the girls an old-fashioned prim dress. After breakfast we children would have to stand around in the hall and wait for Mr Jenton to come and give us 2p each for the church collection. After this money ceremony had been performed, we climbed into the home's minibus. Mr Jenton would drop us off at church and go home, except for the odd occasion when he or his wife sat in on the service.

At church I and some of the other boys would mess about. It was a free-for-all as far as we were concerned. We mucked around, took the piss out of people, made pea-shooters with pens – and that was only the start of it. After the service we were made to go to Sunday school in an old church hall. There was only one adult in charge of the Sunday school and the rest of the people there were young boys and girls, so it was here that the other boys from Highbroom and I really became disruptive. Nothing could stop us because we had no fear of any punishment. Every Sunday at least one or all of us from Highbroom would get told off or thrown out. As time went on our behaviour got worse and worse. In the end we would call the Sunday school teachers bible-bashers and Jesus freaks to their faces. And we would also tell them that we thought church was a load of shit and that we didn't believe in God and all that crap. Once all that was over with we could go home, change into our normal clothes, and for the rest of the afternoon our time was our own.

The meals at Highbroom were pretty meagre and of very poor quality generally. The portions were not really sufficient for growing children, and often I would leave the table feeling hungry. The meals lacked variety and I found them repetitive and bland. Occasionally there were second helpings, but this was rare and usually the food was only left because it was something nobody liked. We had to queue up for a long time by the kitchen and wait our turn to be served. Then we would walk past the rest of the queue to wait in the dining-room. Even when everyone had returned from the kitchen and was seated we couldn't yet begin to eat. First there needed to be silence and then someone would say grace, usually a member of staff, sometimes a child. Throughout grace everyone was meant to be silent, keep their eyes closed and put their hands together in an attitude of prayer. The grace usually went something like this:

Thank you for our food
May the Lord make us truly thankful
Amen.

Sometimes, however, the member of staff would make it up as he or she went along. It was on those occasions that grace went on indefinitely, making us wait even longer for our food. When we were at last permitted to eat it, it was usually stone cold.

One teatime one of the younger children started messing around. Instinctively I said to him, echoing Betty's reproaches to me, 'You little bugger.' Gary, one of the other children, a year or so younger than me, said: 'You can't say words like that, they'll tell you off!'

'What, "bugger"?'

'Yes, it's a swear word,' said Gary.

I told him it was an everyday word, because my foster mum always used to call me it. I then went on to give examples from Betty's extensive repertoire: you little bugger, you're a naughty bugger. Everyone who was sitting around the table thought it hilarious, especially when I checked with the member of staff on duty to see if bugger *was* a swear word. From that day onwards the word bugger was adopted by Gary but modified to 'booger'. From then on many adults and children were called 'booger'.

One Sunday afternoon we went into the dining-room for tea. On each of our plates sat one small tomato. Everyone looked at the tomatoes in astonishment: was this our tea? No, it couldn't be. Surely this was some sort of practical joke? A tomato for tea! Nobody was absolutely sure, though, so we asked the staff. 'Is this all we are getting for tea, one tomato each?'

'Yes, that's your tea.' Then we had to say grace before starting our banquet of one tomato. Some of the younger children were still a bit puzzled about what they should do with the tomato, so they asked the staff, 'What are we supposed to do with it?' We were then all informed that we were to make sandwiches with our one tomato.

The staff were also very strict about the amount of food the children were allowed. On each of the tables in the dining-room was a bowl of sugar and a small butter dish. These were refilled every day, but they had to last two meals, evening tea and breakfast. Because of the measly amount allotted to each table, in the morning there was rarely enough butter or sugar for a reasonable breakfast. Some tables were better at making their microscopic portions go around than others, scrimping at teatime to save it for the morning.

Gary and I sat at the same table so we used to use what sugar and butter we wanted at teatime and replenish the supplies later. One of us kept guard while the other went around the other tables and nicked their butter and sugar. We took it in turns on alternate nights to steal or keep guard. Some mornings when we came down we could hear other children moaning about the disappearance of the butter and sugar they had saved, while some of the children on our table would be surprised to see enough for breakfast. Gary and I would look at each other and pretend not to know what they were talking about. We told the others on our table to keep quiet if they wanted butter and sugar for their breakfast every morning.

The nearest chip shop was a ten-minute walk away. I would often go there in the evenings, not long after teatime, with some of the other kids. We were often still hungry after eating what they dished up at the home. If we had any extra cash we bought a pickled onion to go with the chips. More often than not we wouldn't even have enough pocket-money left for a portion of chips and then we were reduced to buying scraps, the greasy bits of batter and chips left in the bottom of the fryer, for about 5p a bag. On many a cold night we were very glad to have a bag of scraps. The crunchy, oily taste gave you just a hint of the real thing. Sometimes we were so skint that we even had to share a bag of scraps. The chip shop was a godsend, and things would often get really desperate on Sunday and Monday night when it was closed. After a time we became known at the chip shop and were given extra chips, for which we were very grateful.

As Highbroom was out in the countryside you had to walk everywhere, unless you owned a car, motorbike or push-bike. I and the other children at the home had no choice but to walk. Beacon School was a two-mile trudge each way. If it snowed or rained we would still have to walk. Only when it really poured down would the home give us a lift in the minibus. The town of Crowborough was also about two miles from the home, and the railway station was about three miles away. Just down the road was Crowborough Golf Club. We kids often went over there looking for lost golf balls. The idea was that we could sell them to the golfers or the club. Sometimes when we were walking over the golf course, the people playing would lose a ball and ask us to help them to find it, and give us a few bob.

I had been living at Highbroom only a short time before I started smoking. A few of the boys who were about my age said to me one day: 'Come on, we're going for a fag.' I followed them into the grounds, out of sight of staff and other children. We sat down by some trees, one of the boys brought out a packet of cigarettes and we all took one and lit them. I was twelve and hadn't smoked since my last experiment at the age of ten. The cigarette affected me and I felt light-headed and dizzy. It tasted absolutely foul. I didn't enjoy it, but I put on a brave face to the others and pretended everything was fine. Subsequently I began to acquire a taste for nicotine and soon after my first cigarette I bought a packet of fags. Smoking was all part of the macho image and part of the anti-establishment look. It was most definitely outlawed by the staff at Highbroom, which made it all the more attractive to someone like me who opposed the system. When I first started smoking regularly I would be very choosy about which brand of cigarettes I smoked. The brand I adopted was Dunhill International. I liked the taste, I liked the design of the packet, and when smoking them I could pretend to be very posh. However, within a few months I was smoking any brand of cigarettes I could lay my hands on. Smoking became part of my everyday life at Highbroom within a matter of months of my arrival, and it didn't take long for me to get addicted to cigarettes. It was a habit taken up by the boys at Highbroom from the age of about eleven. Not all the boys smoked, but neither were all the girls non-smokers.

Also in a matter of months after arriving I began to get into trouble with the police. It wasn't exactly the crime of the century, but two other boys and I got into trouble for stealing. We hadn't nicked much, but enough in the eyes of the law to warrant a caution at the local police station. I cannot recollect the exact details, or even, come to think of it, how we got caught. Anyway, one of the other children, Gary, was quite well informed about police procedures and told me not to worry. He explained that cautions were simply a little telling off by the Old Bill, and that all you had to say was yes sir, no sir, three bags full sir, and how sorry you were. Armed with this information I wasn't the least bit scared. I knew the score. Mr Edmonds drove us to the police station in Crowborough. He came in with us and we waited until we were called in. None of the others seemed scared by the police station; in fact when we walked past a door bearing the letters CID, I joked to the others, 'Crawling Insects Department,' and we all laughed. Into the sergeant's office we went, all together. He explained what the caution was, told us off and that was it. Gary had been right all along; the caution was no big deal. Once we arrived back at the home we started to act really cool because not only had we been in trouble with the police but we had come away unscathed.

At Highbroom we could be put on punishment for all sorts of reasons, from running away to swearing at staff or even chewing bubble gum. The punishment almost always exceeded the crime. The staff implemented many and various punishments, and more often than not when we were in trouble we would receive a mixture of their favourites, from a telling-off to going without our next meal. They would also stop our pocket-money and when we asked for it they would say it had gone to underprivileged children in Africa. We always suspected they were putting it in their pockets. As the grounds of Highbroom were so vast gardening was a favourite punishment. This was mostly dealt out at weekends, whatever the weather. Clearing and weeding the driveway was another very common penalty. I think the idea was to give any visitors the impression that the grounds were well kept. An alternative gardening punishment was clearing leaves and grass cuttings. There were many times when the staff threatened to put us on punishment by giving us a pair of scissors to cut the grass or a toothbrush to sweep the drive, although I never saw the threat carried out.

On average you would be on punishment for a day or maybe a week, depending on what you had done and who you were. Gary and I spent longer on punishment than most kids. Sometimes we were on indefinite punishment and had absolutely no idea when it would finish. We were never given set hours – you just had to do it until they said you could stop. Being on punishment was hell, and not knowing when it would end made it seem much worse. It was also ridiculous, because it didn't work as a deterrent; it just made us hate the staff even more than we already did. Often when someone was on punishment the other children would buy them sweets out of their own pocket-money. This kind gesture was always much appreciated, especially since the benefactors would be in trouble themselves if they were caught.

Peeling potatoes was not as bad a punishment because although we weren't supposed to use the peeling machine, we occasionally did. However, if we did the job by hand and the peelings were a bit thick we were made to peel the peelings. That aside, we made the most of a bad situation: we could raid the larder if it was unlocked, and we would search the kitchen for things to eat or nick – although there was rarely ever anything worth eating or nicking.

For much of the time that I lived in Highbroom I shared a dormitory with Gary and another boy, Tim, and we soon became good friends. We would smoke together in secret in the grounds of Highbroom, and it was during these illicit sessions that we all got to know one another. Gary had a great sense of humour and made me laugh. He was also very clever and used his intellect when making mischief. Tim was funny too, but quieter than Gary. I didn't get on quite as well with him, although we were still good friends. He was the same age as me, but at school he was in a higher class. We all had a lot of fun together, especially in the dormitory. At night we would talk and mess about pillow-fighting and that sort of thing. After the lights were turned out we were forbidden to talk and were allowed out of bed only to go to the toilet. Often we were caught talking and mucking around. Mr Jenton's accommodation wasn't far from the boys' dormitory and bedrooms so he would go on the prowl to check if anyone was misbehaving. He would burst into the room and quickly slap the offender, or at least the person he assumed was the offender and shout at us to get downstairs. There the punishments were decided: gardening, peeling potatoes or standing facing the wall in silence – that old favourite of Patrick Mitchell's at Domaris.

To get new clothes you had to have some money in your clothing allowance, a set sum of money allocated to an individual annually by Barnardo's. The amount varied according to your age: the older you got, the higher your clothing allowance. I was never told the exact amount of my allowance. There were two major restrictions: first, you always had to have a member of staff with you when you bought new clothes, and secondly, you could only purchase your clothes from one particular shop. The shop where Highbroom held an account in Crowborough was called Cracknall's. Cracknall's was a shop which specialised in school wear and menswear. The menswear was a very down-market version of Dunn and Co. type stuff. Cracknall's clothes were generally old-fashioned, dull, cheap and nasty. Most of the kids who lived near and in Crowborough only shopped in Cracknall's for school uniform, and went elsewhere for casual clothes.

I was forewarned about Cracknall's by the other children long before I was ever taken there. I was given a say in the choice of my clothes, but if it didn't fit in with the member of staff's view I ended up with something else. So when I went to Cracknall's, the name of the game was to try to bargain for the least obtrusive piece of clothing or pair of shoes. The elderly shop assistant had absolutely no idea about fashion, and had a knack of bringing out items that made me want to throw up. He always sided with the staff, no matter what they said. The buying of new clothes became an ordeal – the 'us and them' syndrome again. It was me versus the member of staff and the shop assistant. No matter what I said they always won in the end, and I became the owner of some horrible-looking clothes.

The shoes from Cracknall's came into a category of their own. They were desperately unfashionable and unsightly. The children in Highbroom called the shoes 'Cracknall Groovers'. Whenever somebody came back from Cracknall's with new shoes the children would point at them and shout 'Cracknall Groovers!' On the first day you wore your Cracknall Groovers they were christened, a ceremony which consisted of the other children stamping on them. Sometimes after the christening they still looked new, so we would scuff them on the road and in the dirt. The initiation ceremony served two purposes: it was a defiant act against the system, and, more practically, Cracknall Groovers looked a whole lot better scuffed up.

I disliked going to Cracknall's and being virtually forced into buying unfashionable clothes. I never looked forward to having new clothes – all it meant was more confrontation. The fact that 'they' dictated what clothes you could buy and where you bought them made the whole experience very unenjoyable. The clothes from Cracknall's made the boys from Highbroom stand out – we looked so dated in our Cracknall Groovers. This added notoriety was something we could well have done without.

I spent two Christmases at Highbroom. Christmas at

Highbroom was for me an emotional ordeal. When you are in care you know that for one reason or another you are unwanted or unable to be cared for by your natural parents, but it is at Christmastime that this really hits you. I and about four other children out of around twenty-five were the only ones who remained behind to spend Christmas at Highbroom. I would look at myself and the others and think, we are society's rejects – unwanted, unloved, and in this horrible bloody 'home' for Christmas. No one wants us. No doubt the staff didn't want to spend their Christmas looking after us either, but they were obliged to do it because it was their job.

On Christmas Day only Mr and Mrs Jenton worked. We were treated fairly well, and I daresay they did their best to make it a happy day. We all received a number of presents and had Christmas dinner, and in the evening we were allowed to stay up and watch late-night films. Nobody was hit or given a severe telling-off all day. The Jentons were certainly more lenient and less hostile to us children, but this didn't in any way make me feel better. I knew that the slightly compassionate act was only for the day, and that the usual regime would be back tomorrow. It was during Christmas Day that I came to the conclusion that Christmas was for families, not for unwanted individuals. I hated Christmas, and believed that I could never enjoy such a family-orientated celebration.

I felt much happier when Christmas was over. It wasn't just the fact that I was in a home at Christmas, because I hadn't felt good about Christmas since I was a very small child. No matter where I spent the 'festive' season I felt sad knowing that I never had and never would spend a proper Christmas with my real parents. I hadn't been a child in the full sense of the word since the age of seven, and my memories of Christmas from then were sad ones.

# 11

# Fighting Hard to Survive

My dormitory-mate Tim had been going to Boys' Brigade since long before I moved to Highbroom. He suggested that Gary and I joined. We weren't at all keen but Tim persuaded us by assuring us that we would be taught to play musical instruments. So Gary and I agreed. The staff at the home were very enthusiastic and encouraged us to go. I think they were pleased to get rid of all three of us on the same night and they probably thought the discipline and religious ethos of the organisation would do us good. From the outset I hated Boys' Brigade and so did Gary. Playing soldiers in a musty church hall was not our idea of fun. We thought it best to give it a couple of weeks to see if things would improve, but they didn't. So we asked if we could leave. The man in charge said to give it a couple of weeks, but what was worse was that the staff at Highbroom refused to allow us to leave. Gary and I were really pissed off with the whole thing, for not only was it crap at Boys' Brigade but also we never got to touch a musical instrument although we had been going along for weeks.

We had dug ourselves into a right hole: we'd asked to go to Boys' Brigade but when it didn't live up to our expectations we were not to be allowed to stop. We were being made to go somewhere we didn't want to go in what was supposed to be our free time. Gary and I drew up a plan together. We decided to disrupt the meetings until they threw us out.

Most of the Boys' Brigade uniform was school uniform with odd bits added and some taken away. Our first campaign was not bothering to make sure our uniform looked right for inspection. When it came to handing in subs to a higher-ranking member we would drop the money on the floor, and when he bent down to pick it up we would kick him up the arse. Ironically, the discipline was what made this possible: nobody was allowed to talk or move and there were rows of people in front. Then we would deliberately mess up the marching and drill. That really got them wound up. Also, we would cheat and mess about when it came to games. One of the leaders at Boys' Brigade was also deputy headmaster at Beacon School. He thought that Gary and I would benefit from Boys' Brigade and was prepared to persevere with us. That meant we had to step up our campaign. Just as Gary and I were about to launch into our new and more vigorous plan of action, Tim, who had got us into the mess in the first place, decided he also wanted to leave. We told him the new strategy, which was to do and say what we liked until they had had enough of us.

The new campaign made even the dull Boys' Brigade meetings fun. Swearing at these idiots and taking the piss out of them was a huge joke to us and a big shock for some of the goody-goodies. The new campaign didn't have its desired effect straight away, even when we stole sweets from the tuck shop. But we knew it would come good in the end. The Boys' Brigade held a sponsored walk to raise money for something or other. Gary, Tim and I decided to get the forms for it. We got some people to sponsor us, kept the money and didn't even do the walk; it was an easy little earner for us. Then there was the Christmas Party. We tried very hard to sabotage this by letting off stink bombs. We let them off next to the buffet so that all the food stank of shit. Then we ran out of the hall and down the road. All three of us were in stitches, tears running down our faces, when one of the leaders came after us and made us go back into the hall. He said: 'If we have to put up with the smell, then so do you.' After that we made jokes about the awful smell in the hall, blaming the mouldy food and singling out various people for farting.

Inevitably it all came to a head when we went all-out to get chucked out. Gary, Tim and I would tell people to fuck off and were generally abusive all night so that everyone got the message. All three of us had to have a meeting with a Boys' Brigade leader, the deputy headmaster. We explained to him that we had asked to leave months ago but both the home and he himself had forced us to stay against our will, and that behaving badly was the only way we could see to get out. After a long discussion he agreed to arrange with the home for us to leave. It was a small victory, but I was pleased with it.

At about the same time, I was helping Gary in a scam he had set up at Highbroom. The general idea was that we would sell something to some of the younger children for 50p, say, and demand that they pay us in instalments of 10p per week. The stuff that we sold them was always over-priced and we persuaded the kids to buy things they didn't really want. I had only been involved with the racket a few weeks when I told Gary I thought we should scrap it. I feared that some of the children might tell their older and bigger brothers, which might lead to us getting our heads kicked in, or that they would go and tell the staff that we were ripping them off. More than that, I felt guilty about it. I told Gary that I didn't think we should take pocket-money from the younger kids – we could make much more money by other less risky means. After that the racket ceased.

Being such an old mansion, at Highbroom there were plenty of old ornaments, antique pots, jars and other odds and ends of junk lying about. We reckoned we could put this to good use. A mile or so up the road from the home was a tatty old antique/junk shop. Gary and I put two and two together, and every now and again we would steal something from Highbroom and sell it up the road in the junk shop. It was a way of raising a bit of extra cash on a Saturday afternoon. The owner of the shop was no easy pushover and often gave us a much lower price than we had anticipated for our contraband. I soon became quite good at haggling with him. I would start with a price I knew was ridiculous and we haggled down the figure I expected to get. It was always left up to me to do the haggling in the shop because I looked older than Gary and I was a match for anyone when it came to negotiating. One day I was trying to do a deal in the junk shop when all of a sudden the owner asked me for my National Insurance number. This was a sticky situation. I had no idea what he was on about. I didn't have it on me, I said, and off-hand I couldn't remember it. Then we quickly got out of the shop. So the dismantling of Highbroom's heritage stopped. Apart from anything else, there wasn't much left worth taking and the absence of anything that was any good would soon have been noticed – the remaining pieces were far too big and cumbersome to smuggle out surreptitiously.

We received our pocket-money on Saturdays, and in the afternoon we would go into Crowborough to spend it. It wasn't very much and it didn't last long, so Gary, Tim and I eked it out by stealing what was fairly easy to take and using the money for things that were difficult to nick, such as cigarettes. Saturday afternoons were the highlight of the week. The long walk into Crowborough was never much fun, but once we got into town it was time to have a laugh. There really wasn't much to do in Crowborough, even on a Saturday, but the way we got our kicks was stealing. The adrenaline would be racing around your body long before you actually stole anything. Some shops were so easy that there was no sense of achievement robbing them. Woolworth's was quite an easy target but there wasn't a great deal worth nicking. The sports shop was another of our favourites, although it was far from easy and you had to be a bit sharp; there were plenty of beady-eyed staff to keep an eye on the customers.

Stealing became second nature. It seemed no more strange to steal something than to buy it. We had no set way of working – sometimes I would go in on my own, other times there would be two of us or all three of us at once. When we all went in we would either work individually or as a team, depending on the shop and what we were after. If we worked as a team the proceeds would be roughly shared out, but if we worked on our own sharing wasn't compulsory. Occasionally there were arguments about the spoils of our crimes, but they were few and far between and would be resolved fairly amicably. The gaining of material wealth from crime wasn't what gave the most pleasure, it was 'getting one over on society'. In some strange way I felt I was beating the system; I was conning them, they weren't conning me. I never looked upon stealing from shops as dishonest, more as a bit of harmless fun.

Not far from the school were a sweetshop and a general store. Just after the last bell which signalled home-time they were always packed with school kids anxious to spend their money on sweets, soft drinks and crisps. Very rarely did I or my friends pay for the sweets, crisps and biscuits that we got from either shop. Stealing from them was unbelievably easy; you just went in and took what you wanted. The owners were greedy and liked the shops full of children willing to spend their money on a load of shit that would rot their teeth, and they were always too preoccupied with serving them to keep an eye on the thieving locusts from Highbroom.

After many months of perpetual stealing from the two shops our faces became known so we had to be a little more skilled and sophisticated. The sweetshop started a system whereby they only allowed so many kids in at a time. This reduced the problem but it didn't stop it. Meanwhile, at the general store, thieving went on much as before, although teamwork replaced much of the individual efforts. It was all very much part of our everyday life – to us it seemed fair game. Unlike most events in our lives stealing wasn't regulated by the clock because we could do it at any time of the day or night. After school it provided a bit of excitement before the long walk back to the home. We ate and drank our plunder on our way to the prison Highbroom. If we had had enough and there was some left over we would throw the remainder of the biscuits and crisps at one another. After eating and drinking our fill we would then have a smoke and boast about how cool and clever we were.

Gary, Tim and I even pinched a tape-recorder from Beacon School. It was kept under lock and key in one of the stationery cupboards. Once the other two had nicked it, it was up to me to get it back to Highbroom in case the others were noticed near the scene of the crime. It would have been very risky for Gary and Tim to have been found in possession of the tape-recorder. It wasn't particularly flash – in fact it was very basic – but it had a nice black case with a long shoulder strap. It was a tape-recorder and it was ours.

Once the machine was safely stashed at Highbroom we didn't go near it until Saturday afternoon. Then, together, we went to a quiet place and played some cassettes on our new tape-recorder. Before long it went wrong. Luckily we knew how to fix it but to do so we needed a screwdriver, which we didn't have. So off we all went to the shops, taking the machine with us. Gary and I went into a hardware shop, chose a screwdriver and paid for it. We then fixed the tape-recorder and put it back together out of sight of the shop. Then Gary and I went back to the shop, told the man behind the counter that our father had sent us back with the screwdriver because it was the wrong size and that he would be down later. The man refunded the money. We set off home in a jubilant mood – not only had we mended the tape-recorder but we had managed to fool the shopkeeper into lending us a screwdriver.

After stealing the tape-recorder we began to take things from school regularly. At first we stole from teachers' desks, and books and paper from the stock cupboard. I have no idea why, because we didn't like school work and had absolutely no use for cartons of paper and school exercise books. Then a small group of us began a trick that I was familiar with from primary school – going through the pockets in the school cloakroom. This time though, there was more to be had than just sweets, money and Graham Jones' biscuits. There were calculators, flash pens, watches and all sorts of other unexpected finds. We divided up the spoils in the toilets. It wasn't long before other petty criminals wanted to get involved, and about four or five break-away groups sprang up, all working the cloakrooms around Beacon School. They copied the very safe system that we, the original group, had devised. However, the break-away groups weren't fussy about whom they allowed in, and this was later to cause a great many problems.

The groups were not organised and there was no central control. Each group would just do its own thing, and the thieving was rife. Sometimes Gary and I would go to rob a cloakroom, only to find that it was already being exploited by someone else. This was no real problem because Beacon School was so large and had many cloakrooms. The authorities were quite slow on picking up on this and the cloakrooms and school bags were being systematically robbed every lunchtime. By the time they realised what was going on, it was pretty entrenched. In the school assemblies, announcements were made about robberies around the school, warning people to be vigilant and not to leave valuables in the cloakrooms or their bags. One day as we sat in assembly the teacher announced: 'The Beacon Bag Raiders have struck again!' Our group had never considered giving itself a name and certainly not the Beacon Bag Raiders. We were not into stupid names – all we cared about were the things we nicked. I suppose one of the teachers came up with the name just to make things sound more dramatic. But it gave me and the others a good laugh. Bloody Beacon Bag Raiders, indeed!

Things carried on as before, the announcements about the 'Beacon Bag Raiders' continued, but gradually fewer and fewer valuables were left around for us to find. One afternoon Gary told me that Adrian, a member of a break-away group, was going mad about not getting his fair share and that if something wasn't done about it he was going to grass on every group and everyone he knew to be involved. This was serious. I told Gary to get on to the group and tell them to give Adrian whatever he wanted, anything so long as he kept his gob shut. The group, however, didn't like Adrian. To them he was a horrible little posh wanker who always wanted more than his fair share. Gary spoke to the group but to no avail. They hated Adrian and would not give in to any more of his demands. Adrian, meanwhile, stuck to his word and carried out his threats. We were all in big trouble.

Adrian had gone to a senior teacher and told all he knew about the Beacon Bag Raiders. He knew a lot, and others, less familiar with confronting the authorities, also spoke out once they were put under a little bit of pressure. Gary, Tim and I, the original group members, were rounded up. We were all interrogated individually and that evening after school had finished, the original members and a few others who were involved were sent around the school to gather up all the stolen pens and things that we had thrown away. But even after a very extensive search we were unable to find all the masses of pens and pencil cases that we had discarded over the months. We took back to the teachers what little we had found, knowing full well that was not the last we would hear of it.

That evening the police came to Highbroom. They weren't beat bobbies, but plain clothes coppers from the CID. They arrived in an unmarked dark green Escort, but we knew as soon as we saw them walk in that they were the 'filth'. The two policemen spoke to Mr Jenton before they called Gary, Tim and myself into the room. Gary told us not to worry – they had nothing on us, all we had to do was say nothing. Everything would be all right as long as we said nothing; after all, as Gary said, we had the right to remain silent. We all knew what to do and had to stick together. If anyone spoke we would all be implicated.

Gary was the first to be called into the sitting-room for questioning. I sat waiting for what seemed like an eternity in the familiar gloom of Highbroom. The hairs on the back of my neck prickled and my palms were damp, yet it was not fear I felt – Gary's advice had proved right the last time we had run up against the police – it was a rush of adrenaline preparing me for stonewalling their questions. By now the contempt for authority I had developed almost overnight when I was dumped at the home had become a permanent part of me.

Tim was called in, and Gary emerged to tell me how his ordeal had gone. From what I could gather from his whispers they had given Gary a very hard time, but Gary was an old hand with the police and police procedure. He had handled himself well and come out of his interrogation feeling reasonably OK. At last it was my turn. The two policemen eyed me coldly and told me to sit down. Somehow their ordinary clothes made them more intimidating than their uniformed counterparts. Mr Jenton sat to one side, silent. I was determined I wouldn't say a word to those bastards.

The questioning began, first about school, then about home, and then about stealing from shops. Yes, I said I had done some thieving at school but I admitted nothing else. Time went on and I was still not saying what they wanted to hear.

'Well, if you don't talk we will just have to put you down for some of our unsolved cases of burglary and TDA [taking and driving away].' I could hardly believe my ears. Me, do a burglary or nick cars? This copper was obviously talking out of his arse. I thought, what a bastard, threatening to put all that on me. I got the message all right, but there was no way I was telling them anything. My interrogation came abruptly to an end.

But there was more to come. Tim was the first to go in for the second interrogation. Meanwhile Gary and I discussed the situation and realised that things had taken a turn for the worse. Tim was in for a long time. When he came out of the sitting-room, white-faced, he looked very shaken up. They had obviously given him a hard time. I didn't get a chance to speak to Tim before being commanded by Mr Jenton to go into the sitting-room for my second interrogation. I could feel that things had stepped up a gear. The atmosphere was highly charged and menacing. I wasn't offered a seat. I stood before the policemen. The questions were similar to the first ones that I hadn't answered. The difference was in the attitude of the coppers, who became more and more hostile towards me.

The next thing I knew I felt a punch in my stomach. A hand hit my face and I lost my balance as I was shoved, hard, across the room. I fell against the wall, winded and shocked. I recovered quickly from the shock but the bastard was still pushing me against the wall and punching and slapping me. After a few minutes the beating stopped and I was given a seat.

I sat down. I was astounded at what had just occurred. I was completely out of my depth. I didn't know the script for this scene and had no idea what would happen next. I had never felt so vulnerable in my whole life. Mr Jenton, the head of the home, had just sat and watched me take a beating from a policeman and had raised neither voice nor hand to protect me. No one gave a shit about me, the coppers could do what they liked. Frightened, crying and shaking, I then, at last, answered their bloody questions. I was in no state to make a protest. I would say and do whatever was necessary as long as it brought the nightmare to an end. The other copper, not the one who had beaten me up, took down my statement. I told them about every last paltry item I had stolen since living in Crowborough, plus all the crimes I had been involved in as the decoy up front while the others helped themselves to goods in shops. That night I would have signed my own mother's death warrant, had I known who she was, if I thought it could bring a quick end to the horror. When the police started taking down my statement Mr Jenton went out of the room, returning a few minutes later with a tray in his hands. On the tray were three cups of coffee and a large plate of biscuits. Not any old biscuits: no, these were assorted chocolate biscuits, the expensive type we children never got to see. Mr Jenton took a cup of coffee from the tray and resumed his posture, arms folded, a horrible smug look on his ugly face. He had sat there with that self-satisfied smug look on his face while I'd been beaten. It was as if he enjoyed watching me being knocked about.

Gary went in after me for a dose of the same treatment. When I came out of the sitting-room I was shaking with fear and fury. I hated adults even more than I had before. They were all bastards, the whole lot of them.

Once the interrogations had finished the two coppers went up to our bedroom and turned the place over. All our meagre possessions were strewn across the bedroom floor and quite a lot of things were smashed or torn up. Judging by the mess you would have thought there'd been a riot in our room. After the police left we were sent to our bedroom to tidy up the mess that the bastards had left and then we were sent to bed.

Very soon after the police visit to Highbroom the three of us were summonsed to appear in court. Mr Jenton drove us there. The only good thing about it was that we had the morning off school. I had never been to court before – Gary and Tim had – and I didn't know what to expect. It was 10 May 1977, and I was twelve years old. When we arrived at Marks Cross Juvenile Court it was nine o'clock in the morning. Outside we met Gary's dad and uncle, and then Tim's mum turned up. Gary and I were surprised when we saw her because she was so young. Just then Jim Johnson, my social worker, appeared. It was scant consolation. I couldn't have cared less whether he was there or not. I felt like shit. I was bereft of any support, moral or otherwise.

All the adults went in before us. We had to wait outside till we were called. Gary went off to the toilet and came back with a stolen mirror, a show of bravado that lifted our spirits. We were talking among ourselves, making the most of a bad situation, when a court official came up. 'I wouldn't be so happy if I were in your place,' he said. 'If I were you lot I would keep quiet.' We made some reply to the effect that he wasn't in our place and we couldn't give a fuck anyway. Then it was time to go in.

We walked into the court room slowly. Inside I glanced around. It wasn't that big, but it looked quite bleak and official. Everyone except the relatives and Jim was seated behind tables. Behind us sat Gary's uncle and father, Tim's mother and Jim. At that moment I wanted to die. Everyone else had some family members there except me. I had a poxy social worker. I felt so cold and unwanted. The only person who was there to support me was a person who was paid for doing so. I didn't feel like a human being, I felt like a hollow institutional object – and one that even the institution had rejected, at that. I felt too angry to be intimidated. At that moment in time I wanted to smash everyone and everything in that court room. The bastards humiliating me like this. I wanted to wreck the place and tell them they couldn't do this to me. I kept control somehow and calmed down a little, although I did make a small protest: I pushed some papers and paperclips on to the floor. How I kept that one small act of defiance from turning into a more violent unleashing of my feelings I don't know.

Before the proceedings started everyone was asked if they wanted a man removed from the court as he was known to be a friend of Mr Jenton. No one did. I would have done, but I didn't want them to label me as some sort of troublemaker. The court room was full of adults, and although they weren't wearing wigs and gowns I couldn't help thinking how nasty they all looked. We were the corpses, they were the hungry vultures. The magistrate was a middle-aged, middle-class woman who looked very stern indeed. The proceedings began.

We were told why we were there, who everyone was and what the procedure was. To start with our statements were read out in turn, and Gary, Tim and I had to say whether or not the statements were true. Our parents or guardians had to confirm this. Some of the statements were quite lengthy, especially mine, so that part took a long time. Under my breath I repeated, bastards, bastards, fucking bastards, bastards, fucking bastards. When the proceedings had finished we were shown out of the court room while the panel came to a decision. We were kept waiting for about half an hour before going back in to hear our fate.

Tim was first. The verdict was read out, and then his punishment, which was a fine of £25. Then my verdict was read out; the charges had included aiding and abetting which, in the eyes of the law, is worse than stealing. My punishment was a £40 fine. Gary's was £37. I couldn't believe it. Why was I fined the most? Forty bloody quid! We were all as guilty as each other. Bastard magistrate, bastard panel, forty bloody quid. Justice? Bullshit more like. Then the magistrate told us that if she ever saw any of us in her court again we would be sent to a detention centre. She thought she was hard but I couldn't have cared less about her threat. She might as well have said, 'I will transfer you from one prison to an even worse prison.' I was unimpressed. DC, that didn't frighten me. I didn't care about anything any more. In Highbroom you got used to being treated like shit. These dickheads thought themselves so hard having a go at me, just because I had no family to help and support me. What I did wasn't good but giving me the highest fine, well, that was criminal.

Once the magistrate had finished her summing up we left the court room. Gary and Tim spoke to their families for a few minutes. I said very little to my social worker. Then we were driven back to Highbroom for dinner before school in the afternoon. Gary, Tim and I worked out a plan of action to get some money together to pay off the fines. We would do a runner down to Dymchurch and work there on the fair and pay off the fines in one big lump sum. Gary and Tim were setting off after lunch and not going into school that afternoon, and it was arranged that I would meet them after school.

That afternoon everyone in my class wanted to know all the details. I told them all I could remember and most of the class were shocked that I should have got the biggest fine. It probably looked as if I was the worst of the group or the leader, neither of which was true. As soon as I got back to Highbroom after school I prepared to escape.

The bike that was to be my getaway vehicle had no brakes, no lights and no mudguards. It was a very basic contraption and belonged to Roger Mason, a boy at the home. I didn't own so much as an inner-tube. Roger's brother, Tony, wanted to go with us for some reason. Tony and I hadn't got twenty yards from Highbroom before I had my first crash. I swerved to miss a fast and badly driven car and ended up in a holly bush. Luckily I wasn't injured, just a bit shaken. The driver didn't stop to see if I was OK or not. As soon as I was back on the bike we were off, pedalling hard and fast. When we all met up everyone was in jubilant mood. We were on our way to Dymchurch.

Back at Highbroom, Roger Mason had worked himself into a right old state. His brother had run away on his best bike and I had gone off with his reserve bike. He had run out of Highbroom, fuming, and hailed a car, coincidentally the very car that had nearly crashed into me. Roger explained the situation to the driver, jumped in and off they drove, in hot pursuit of the runaway cyclists.

Needless to say, the four of us hadn't got far before they caught us up. They drove us off the road and into the hedgerow. When Roger and the driver got out a momentous argument ensued, which came very close to a punch-up. In the end we had no choice but to go back peacefully – otherwise they would have called the police.

We all thought that Roger had been a real creep and had messed up everything. His attitude towards his bikes was very childish. What I couldn't understand was why he was getting so worked up about the death trap I was on. When we got back to Highbroom it was trouble all round – except for Roger, that is. He was giving it the big hero bit. All we had wanted to do was pay off our fines, however unjust they were. We wanted to pay them as quickly as possible and pay them our way.

# 12

# Mum and Dad

That same year I asked my social worker about my parents. I wanted to know about them and to visit them. He was very vague and clearly reluctant to tell me anything. In the end I managed to find out that they lived in Kent and that my father worked for the council. I desperately needed to see my mum and dad. Although they had visited me when I was a baby I was too young to remember. I would kid myself that my mum and dad were famous and I was illegitimate, and that one day they would see the error of their ways and come to collect me. Another thing I would tell myself was that I was the child of a royal family, but because I was illegitimate no one would claim me. My imagination knew no boundaries because I had had no real facts about my mum and dad to go on for the thirteen years of my life. Consequently I came up with loads of weird and wonderful ideas about them.

It was more than a natural curiosity. I was more desperate than ever before to find my parents. Once I had joined them, I could go home at last and escape from my horrendous life in care. They were my last and only hope, for I knew that if I didn't find them I would never escape institutional life. It never occurred to me that my mum and dad might have been unsuitable parents. I suppose this was because they were my dream, the dream that kept me alive when things got bad. I never thought ill of them except for having put me into care. I had a picture in my mind of roses around a door and a warm, homely house inside, and a perpetual hope that one day I would go there, to the loving arms of my mother and father. That dream was still with me in 1977, and because of it I kept on at my social worker to take me to see them.

Jim was against it. I protested that I had a right to see them. Eventually he relented, warning me that he didn't want to take me and he didn't think it was a good idea. At about that time my mother was writing letters to Barnardo's demanding my return. My social worker told me about the letters and I said that I must see my parents so that I could decide whether or not I wanted to go there to live.

The big day arrived at last. I was going to meet my parents. I had been looking forward to this day all my life and today was the day. All the dreams, hopes and aspirations of thirteen years came together in the concentrated knot in the pit of my stomach. I was far too wound up to sleep the night before. I had never been so excited in my life. At last, I had a glimpse of the light at the end of the tunnel.

Jim Johnson came to Highbroom and picked me up just after breakfast. The journey seemed to take forever. I couldn't believe this was really happening. Very little was said in the car but when we arrived outside my parents' house Jim turned off the engine and spoke to me quietly. He advised me not to expect too much, and warned me that I might be a bit shocked by what I found.

We approached the front door. I was almost shitting myself for I knew that behind that door were my mother and father. The parents I had dreamed of seeing for thirteen long years were now only seconds away. There was no turning back. My social worker knocked on the door.

A few seconds later the door opened. There in front of me stood a short, poorly dressed old woman who bore no resemblance to me. My first sight of my mother was to be one of the biggest shocks of my life.

We entered the house, and my mother started to talk. I couldn't believe my ears. She spoke like a retarded child. Immediately I knew she was mentally subnormal. It was too much to take in. I was in a state of severe shock. The house looked as if nothing much had changed since the 1920s. The furnishings were old and tatty, it was dirty and the lighting was dim. In the grate I noticed an original pair of bellows. Above the mantelpiece was a big, heavy wooden-framed mirror, on either side of which hung huge photographs of my grandparents. Everywhere I looked there were photographs. Quite a lot were of men in uniform, mostly from the First World War, and some from the Second. The kitchen was cluttered with battered old utensils and there was washing hanging above the table.

I remember that vividly, because although it hung on a line it was dirty. The whole house, and especially the kitchen, smelt like an old junk shop. The smell got into your throat and nose like the smell of smoke from a blazing fire. I don't remember the upstairs of the house, except that there were two bedrooms, one of which I was told would be my room when I came home to live.

My social worker said something to my mother about some papers my dad had to sign. 'Oh, I will have to sign them – Mr Fever can't write,' she replied. I thought to myself, my father can't write his own name? This isn't really happening, it's all a horrible nightmare. I had been told that my father worked for the council, so I imagined he worked in an office. But I discovered later that he was illiterate and worked as a gardener. Before that he had been a dustman and a road-sweeper. Jim left after a few minutes, leaving my mother and I to have a nice little chat. He would pick me up later. I didn't know what to say. There I was in a strange house with a mentally ill old woman who was supposed to be my mother. I said very little. I was at a complete loss. After only minutes in my parents' house thirteen years of hopes and dreams had started to disintegrate. I knew it would never be my home or sanctuary from institutional life.

It simply couldn't be true. My only chance of escape did not exist, had never existed. I felt physically ill and emotionally devastated. I had been conned. The bastards. This wasn't my mother, this wasn't my parents' home. They had done this deliberately so that I wouldn't get any ideas about leaving care. The bastards!

My father had not even bothered to take the day off work so

I never saw him that fateful day. It was probably just as well – I had had more than enough shocks for one day.

Later Jim came to pick me up. I was relieved to get out of the house. 'Why didn't you tell me what my mother was like?' I asked. He said something to the effect that they didn't want to upset me and hoped that I wouldn't want to see my parents after all this time. I wanted to have a go at my social worker but decided not to, in case he wouldn't co-operate with my wishes regarding my parents. I was extremely angry that I had been totally unprepared for what was to be one of the biggest shocks of my life. I truly believed that it had been handled this way deliberately.

What I had dreamt of as being my salvation was to be my living nightmare. Even so, in spite of everything, I still wanted to know more. I had been denied the truth for so long and then, more than ever before, I wanted to know everything about my mum and dad.

My social worker still wasn't very forthcoming but he did tell me about my half-brothers. He told me that my mother had been married before my father, and that she had had two sons by her first husband, and that both of the children had died very young. He said that one died of cot death and the other because my mother fed the baby the wrong food. That night when I got back to Highbroom, I thought constantly about my parents. I cried myself to sleep, thinking that my mother was a murderer who had killed my half-brothers. I wanted to die.

Some time passed and I wanted to see my mother again and meet my father. I needed to find out more. I had to know more – after all, these strange people were said to be my parents, although I still had my doubts. I had to find some way to make sense of it all. Towards the end of 1977 I went to visit my parents and meet my father for the first time. He wasn't quite as I had imagined. For a start he seemed far too old to be my dad and I couldn't believe that he really was. His clothes were dirty, his face unshaven and his speech very inarticulate. Nevertheless, he came across as a caring person and I think he was capable of loving me.

During the second visit to my parents' house I had tea there. The meal, if you could call it that, consisted of cheese and crackers. The crackers were Jacob's and the cheese was English cheddar, washed down with tea. It was one of the oddest meals I've ever had. My parents didn't use ordinary milk, they used tinned Carnation milk. Before tea I had been shown the family photograph albums. There were a lot of photographs, most of which had been taken many years before I was born. I never felt for one moment that I was looking at my forebears, but at some very strange history books without any text. I came away that day feeling as though things weren't as bad as I had first thought. After the initial shock had blown apart my dreams, I clutched at the tattered remains of my desire for my real family. I felt sure that if both my parents and I worked at it, we might be able to get along with one another. I still believed that something could be salvaged and that we would one day get to know one another.

Back at Highbroom I was still getting into trouble. One Saturday afternoon I was walking up the road which led to the home when I saw a garage door wide open. Inside I could see at least two racing bikes. I told Gary and Tony Mason about my find and we knew we had to have them. All three of us went down to the garage and checked out the situation. Although the house was only yards away from the home, it looked like a piece of cake. In the garage stood three bikes: two racing bikes and a girl's bike. It had been decided that as I was the least competent cyclist I should ride the girl's bike. I thought this very unfair as I had found them in the first place. After a brief argument I agreed to ride the girl's bike, a decision that I would come to regret. Only yards away from the garage, I discovered that my prize had a flat tyre, a slow puncture. I got into a real strop and cursed the other two for getting the racing bikes. Gary and Tony were taking the piss out of me because I was on a girl's bike, but when they realised what was wrong it wasn't so funny. We all knew that it would slow us down, and time was vitally important.

Once well away from the scene of the crime, we needed to decide what to do next. We came to the conclusion that it would be far too risky to ride about on the bikes in case someone saw us, so we hid them in the field near the home, planning to get some spray paint later to disguise them. That night every child in Highbroom was summoned to the hall. Mr Jenton was in a very bad mood indeed. He had received a phone call from the people across the road saying that three bikes had been stolen from their garage that afternoon and that they suspected the kids from the children's home and wanted Mr Jenton to investigate. After Mr Jenton's initial speech about how he wanted the culprits to come forward he dismissed everyone – except Gary, Tim and myself. I can't quite remember what exactly happened but I think Tony owned up and Tim was let off. The three of us who had nicked the bikes stood in the hall, while Mr Jenton gave us a severe telling-off and told Tony that he should know better than to get mixed up with the likes of Fred and Gary. Then we were told to go and fetch the bikes, along with a couple of other boys who were a bit more trustworthy than us. We were given torches to help us find them because it was pitch black outside. Twenty minutes later we were back with the bikes. Mr Jenton then put them away somewhere safe and sent us to bed.

Early the next morning, while everyone else was having their breakfast, Gary, Tony and I were in the driveway cleaning up the bikes before they went back to their owners. It was a glorious sunny Sunday morning. 'I know,' said Gary, 'let's do a runner on the bikes.' It was an excellent idea, but I couldn't go because of the flat tyre. Tony and Gary, however, warmed to the idea and laid their plans. 'Carry on cleaning, and when I count to three, drop the rags, jump on and pedal like fuck,' said Gary. On the count of three they were off down the drive like lightning. A few minutes later Mr Jenton came out.

'Where are they?'

I said I didn't know.

'Which direction did they take?'

I said I hadn't seen.

The girl's bike was taken back to the neighbours, who were far from pleased, and later that day Gary and Tony were picked up by the police in Brighton. On their way they had had a collision and had done some damage to the bikes. They were later charged with stealing them and had to pay for the damage. Some of the children asked me why I hadn't gone on the run, and I told them I would have done had it not been for the flat tyre.

The church we attended had planned a trip to go and see Cliff Richard in concert. The staff at the home got tickets for all of the children, most of whom didn't want to go. But we had no say in the matter of our entertainment. We all had to get dressed in our Sunday best. We boarded the coach, along with the rest of the congregation, on a lovely summer evening. Some of the trippers were excited about seeing Cliff Richard. Most of us from Highbroom felt embarrassed to be with the bible-bashers going to see Cliff Richard.

The theatre was huge and very posh. On the backs of some of the seats were tiny pairs of binoculars which you paid to hire. The charge wasn't much but not many of us had any money left that evening. Those who had squabbled for a seat near the binoculars so that they could hire them and then steal them afterwards. I know of at least one pair of binoculars that found its way back to Highbroom.

The concert was immensely boring. I became restless about halfway through and went off to the loos. Even the bogs were posh. While I sat there, passing the time, I noticed there were plenty of spare toilet rolls, soft, and in a pretty pink shade. For a laugh I decided to decorate the loo with them. I made a really good job of it and it took a long time and a lot of loo paper. By the time I had finished the toilet looked like a pink Christmas grotto. I went back and told Gary, who went off to look at my handiwork. When he clapped eyes on it he was in hysterics. He was gone for some time, and when he returned there were two fairy grotto cubicles in the toilets. When Gary came back and sat down we had a good laugh together, trying to imagine the face of the next person who went into the loos.

By then the concert was coming to a close and some of the children were still trying desperately to pull the binoculars off the back of the seats.

Whenever we could afford to travel to Tunbridge Wells, we did so. It was the nearest decent town to Crowborough where you could buy clothes, records and other such things. There were also cafés and restaurants where Gary and I would go when on a day out there. Nearly all the trips we made to Tunbridge Wells were on a Saturday afternoon when we had our pocket-money. The bus fares were quite expensive, so in order to have a worthwhile afternoon out you needed a few quid in your pocket.

One Saturday in Tunbridge Wells I bought a trilby hat in Dunn and Co. It cost me a lot of money, but I wanted it badly – it was very fashionable at the time to wear a trilby. When I got back to Highbroom that evening Mr Jenton confiscated it. He never did give it back. I'm sure he kept it for himself. Gary and I looked forward to our trips to Tunbridge Wells. They meant getting out of the stifling atmosphere of Highbroom and the boredom of Crowborough for a few hours with no one around to tell us what to do. It was the nearest thing we had to freedom.

At school the friends I made were mostly kids in my form. Nearly all of them were people the teachers saw as trouble-makers or no-hopers; as outcasts for one reason or another. Outside of school I had no friends except for some from the home, and some from Pine Wood, Crowborough's local authority mixed home for girls and boys of different ages. I and others from Highbroom got on really well with them and there was no rivalry between homes, although we did play football against each other. I became good friends with about four or five children from Pine Wood. It was great to meet and talk to other children from a home. They shared your kind of background and problems. Because you all had so much in common you felt less isolated. I think we all gained a great understanding of our feelings.

As well as thieving I had other means of making money. This I did with a certain degree of entrepreneurism at school during breaktime and lunchtime. When autumn came conkers were very much in fashion at Beacon School and demand for good-quality conkers was high. At Highbroom, on the front lawn, stood a huge horse chestnut tree which yielded a good many conkers each year. Some of us gathered loads of conkers and bagged them up in bread bags to sell at school the next day. We put all the small poor-quality conkers at the bottom and all the large good ones at the top of the bag. I sold them for 50p a bag and £1 a bag if the buyer wanted string and a skewer. The skewers I got from the butcher's, and they didn't cost anything.

Another of my business enterprises at school was selling Ovaltine. The home had been donated boxes and boxes of Ovaltine in small sachets. It was so old that all the powder had stuck together to form a small, chewy bar. The taste was not unpleasant, so I nicked a few boxes of Ovaltine from the larder and took them to school. I sold them for 1p each and by the end of one day I had sold £1.95 worth of Ovaltine. But stories of my business acumen got back to Mr Jenton, and I was hauled up before him. I admitted what I had done and he made me hand over the cash. Surprisingly, he didn't give me a real bollocking. I think he was secretly glad to have got rid of some of those old Ovaltines. Selling stuff to other kids at school not only earned me money: it also gave me a sense of achievement because I had made money from nothing through my own ideas.

For a few weeks on Saturday mornings a group from Highbroom went swimming at Beacon School. The school swimming pool wasn't anything special but it made a good break from the usual uneventful Saturday mornings. One day after our swim we found ourselves in the changing-room alone, just us from Highbroom: Gary, his brother Jimmy, Tim and myself. We agreed not to take the opportunity to steal anything from any of the coats left there by the other swimmers: it would have been rather obvious who the culprits were. But for Tim the temptation was just too great, and he took it upon himself to go through a few pockets. Not only did he nick some cash but he also took a watch. The rest of us from Highbroom wanted nothing to do with it – we knew it was very risky and we had not that long ago been in court. In any case, nobody trusted us and we would be the first ones to be questioned if there was any trouble, no matter what it was and even if we were fifty miles away at the time.

By the time we arrived back at the home, the school had already phoned up about the stolen money and watch. We were all immediately given a severe bollocking even though we all protested our innocence. All of us, except Tim, were telling the truth. However, we wouldn't grass on a friend – that wasn't the way we did things, and because of our strong principles we paid a very high price sometimes. Our punishment was a beating with a ruler and no pocket-money. The best bit about it all was when Mr Edmonds hit Gary with the ruler. It broke in half, which we all found highly amusing. I don't think Mr Edmonds saw the funny side, though: it made him look like a right dickhead.

After our telling-off and beating we were put on punishment. Gary, his brother and I were put to work in the grounds while Tim was detailed to the kitchen. Gary chatted as we tidied up the drive. We discussed the whole episode and came to the conclusion that it was very unfair and that we didn't want to do another stroke of work when we were innocent. It was late June and I had recently had a birthday. Gary suggested going on the run. I agreed it would be the only way of getting out of the punishment for a crime we hadn't committed. We could use my remaining birthday money for food and thumb a lift to Brighton or wherever. I had one small reservation – I didn't think it would be a good idea to go without our coats. Although it was summer the weather was pretty indifferent and the nights were cold. Jimmy, Gary's younger brother, appeared and we told him what we were going to do. He wanted to come with us. We agreed, on the condition that he retrieved our coats from the cloakroom without being seen by any staff or children.

A few minutes later we were in our coats and out of the drive.

Once clear of the home we realised that getting a lift for the three of us would be no easy task. I had an idea. We could walk at medium pace, with me at the back pretending to have a bad leg. Gary could walk in the middle and Jimmy, being the youngest and smallest, at the front with his thumb out. Although I was tall and looked older, an injury might gain sympathy. Besides, Jimmy and I would detract attention from Gary in the middle. Our story was going to be that we had missed our bus back to Lewes and that we needed to get home because our parents would be worried. We decided to say Lewes rather than Brighton because it sounded more feasible. Gary and Jimmy thought that my plan was a bit silly but went along with it. There was no harm in trying.

Twenty minutes later we got a lift from an oldish couple in a big car. We got into the back, and told them the story we'd rehearsed. The woman did most of the talking, asking us why we were such a long way from home. We said we had been visiting friends. She seemed satisfied, and gave us some sweets.

Not far into Lewes we asked to be dropped off near a bus stop. We said we lived just up the road and this would do us nicely. We then thanked them for the lift and sweets, got out and walked up the road, pretending to go home. Within a couple of minutes we were back where they had dropped us off.

We were all pleased about the success so far of the bunk. We walked on for a couple of miles, and began to feel tired and hungry – we had gone without lunch as part of our punishment. At the next row of shops we came to we bought a loaf of bread, two pints of milk and some chips. The chip butties, washed down with milk, made us feel a lot better, but after we had finished eating we were all a bit bloated and lethargic so we went and got a bus into Brighton. At the bus shelter we came across a newspaper, which we took with us – it would come in handy for fires and toilet paper.

When we got to Brighton we didn't do much, just dossed about and had a laugh. But the time passed quickly and it wasn't long before it got dark. We then had to decide what to do about Jimmy. He was very young and a liability, really. Gary and I thought it would be best to send Jimmy to their parents, who lived just outside Brighton, a short bus journey away. Gary took Jimmy down to the Old Steine, put him on a bus and paid his fare. When Gary came back we went for some more chips and wandered around the town. As time ticked by, the air cooled and Brighton seemed to be crawling with police cars and vans. This we could do without. We crouched for some time in a telephone box, trying to keep warm and out of sight. The police were everywhere you looked. At about ten o'clock we thought we'd better move on to somewhere quieter than Brighton. We had had enough of crouching in the phone box: our limbs were stiff and we were tiring.

We hadn't got further than a couple of streets from Church Hill Square before two huge policemen appeared in front of us. They asked where we were going. To a mate's place, we said, down there, and pointed down a street. One of the policemen said: 'You're Fred Fever and you're Gary Jones.' Then it was arms up the back and we were pushed into a police van. There were about four or five coppers in the van, plus the driver. Inside we were made to empty our pockets. First out came vast amounts of newspaper, then sweet papers and then finally my remaining money. The coppers looked at all the scrunched-up newspaper, mystified. 'What's all this for?'

'To wipe my arse on,' I calmly replied.

They asked where I got the money from. I told them it was my birthday money. Then it was Gary's turn to empty his pockets. Again out came tons of scrunched-up newspaper and again the coppers said, 'What's this for?'

'The same as his,' replied Gary.

The van lurched through the Brighton streets and pulled up at the nick. Neither of us was handcuffed, so as we got out of the van a copper said to us: 'Don't try doing a runner because we are quick on our feet and we will kick your heads in.' We went in without any trouble. The police put us in a cell, where we were to wait until Mr Edmonds came down from the home to collect us.

Meanwhile, Gary's dad turned up, and he was let out for about ten minutes to talk to his father. Apparently his dad was a bit annoyed and upset, probably because Jimmy had been involved: Jimmy was only nine or ten. After he had gone Gary and I sat around in the cell and waited to be taken back to Highbroom. We weren't troubled by being in a cell – there didn't seem a great deal of difference between that and Highbroom. We had no regrets, except that we hadn't got out of Brighton before the police moved in.

Mr Edmonds wasn't in a very good mood when he came to pick us up, and consequently the journey back to Crowborough wasn't nearly as interesting as the one to Brighton. He complained about the trouble we had caused him and told us that we would have to pay the petrol money. We protested that none of this would have happened had he listened to us and not punished us for something we hadn't done. He couldn't make us pay for the petrol because we didn't have any pocket-money – it was being kept back each week to pay off our court fines. We refrained from asking him how the gardening was going, and whether he had nearly finished.

At the start of the school summer holidays in July 1977, Mr Edmonds asked if I would like to go out for a ride in the van. Many of the other children who lived in Highbroom were going home for the summer to be with their families. Because the majority of children lived along the Sussex coast it made economic sense to drop them off in the home's van, rather than give them all train fares.

That Friday night the kids travelling to the coast eagerly climbed into the van, each carrying some clothes in a bag. Except me. I was just going for the ride. For a change everyone was in a jubilant mood. All were in high spirits – they were going home for a holiday. Not all the children would stay at home for the whole of the summer – some were going for only a couple of weeks – but they were all departing on the same day.

Outside Brighton the van stopped and dropped a few of

them off, and again on the outskirts we dropped another two children. Then Mr Edmonds drove on to Worthing to deliver the last two brothers to their family. The excited voices had gone and a depressing silence reigned in the van. We turned round and headed back to Crowborough. Going along for the ride had been a mistake. It only brought my own situation into sharper focus. The black thoughts that washed over my mind became more intense as we drove inexorably towards Crowborough. I would never be dropped off at home for the summer holidays, or any holiday; I had no real home to be dropped off at. As Crowborough got closer and closer I started to feel physically ill. I would soon be dropped at my 'home', Highbroom. I couldn't get away from the fact that I was an institutional child and totally dependent on charity. I never again went out in the van when the children were dropped off for holidays. I couldn't bear going through the mental ordeal again.

My holiday was to be with Mr and Mrs Edmonds. We stayed in a caravan on a farm in North Wales. There were about four other children and the Edmonds' daughter. None of the other children was a close friend of mine and I didn't have anyone to go around with. I made the most of it though, and had quite a reasonable time. It was a vast improvement on Highbroom and the Edmonds were in a holiday mood and more relaxed. I don't remember getting into any serious trouble, which made a change. The highlight of the holiday came when Mr Edmonds took us to a couple of football matches. We saw Wrexham play and that was quite a good game. Then came the best treat of all: he took us to see Liverpool versus Newcastle, Liverpool's first home game of the new season. I thoroughly enjoyed myself – going to Anfield was the best experience I had had in a very long time. I'd never seen a top club play or been to such a huge stadium before. It was certainly the best part of the holiday.

Not long after I had moved to Highbroom I had got to know some older children. Whenever you move into a new or different institution it takes time before you are fully accepted –

months, or even a year – and some people always remain outsiders. By the time I had been living at Highbroom for a year I had been accepted as one of them. It was because I had gained the trust of the older children that they took me to the pub. I was only thirteen at the time, and although I was quite tall I certainly didn't look eighteen. So when we went to the pub I would sit in the corner out of sight of the bar staff and try to be as inconspicuous as possible. After about three or four trips to the pub I became quite confident, so much so that I went up and bought a drink. I couldn't believe how easy it was. They served me my drink and no questions were asked. After that I decided to see if I could get away with it in other places.

There were two supermarkets in Crowborough. I would go to one of them in my lunch hour, in my school uniform, to buy some cheap biscuits. In the very same supermarket I would buy cans of lager on Saturdays, and it wasn't unknown for the same person to be on the till. Again, just like the pub, it was easy, no questions asked.

My next test was the off-licence. Again I was served without comment. I thought being able to buy booze at thirteen was just great; I had conned loads of adult idiots. I could get hold of drink as and when I wanted it. There was only one small problem: money. I could rarely afford alcohol because most of my money went on cigarettes and chips. However, word soon got around that I could get served in off-licences and pubs and other children, some older, some younger, would ask me to go and buy booze for them. Of course I would do this for a price: either they had to give me some of the booze or some cigarettes. Although I drank very regularly I didn't drink that much – it didn't take much to get me out of my head. I would get drunk as often as I could. I think the staff at Highbroom suspected something but they never said anything to me about drinking. I always made sure I never went back to the home drunk.

# 13

# Some Changes Come About

Soon after starting at Beacon School I began to get thrown out of classes. I was expelled from lessons with such regularity that I didn't need to bunk off. For some classes, I saw no point in turning up in the first place because it was so unlikely that I would complete the whole lesson without being sent out. I don't know what the teachers were trying to achieve by throwing me out. If it was meant as a punishment it didn't work. I didn't mind being ejected – it only reinforced my belief that school was a waste of time and that I could never get anything out of it except more aggravation. Being thrown out of the bottom class meant that there was nothing more the teachers could do to you, except, of course, expel you from the school. I suppose I did feel a bit rejected after a while, but I had come to expect rejection by the authorities as normal: nobody wanted me, that was the way it was. Two could play at that game: I was rejecting them as surely as they rejected me. I finished up not giving a shit whether I was in a lesson or not.

By the time I was in the fourth year the teachers had given up on me. It no longer mattered what I did or how much I achieved, they weren't really interested in me. All they wanted was a quiet life and this was easy to achieve by sending me out of the class. I didn't want to be there, the teachers didn't want me there, I didn't want the lessons, they didn't want to teach me. It was a recipe for confrontation. I didn't loathe all the teachers at Beacon School – there were about two or three whom I respected. Those few individuals treated me as a human being with feelings and not as an object to ridicule and discard.

One day I was in a lesson, for once, and the teacher was having a go at me. He said that I thought I was clever but the truth was, I wasn't, and that I had no power or influence over him or the class. I thought about that and waited for an opportunity to prove him wrong. When it next came to his lesson I set off the fire alarm. The class was evacuated and everyone in the school filed out into the playground. We all stood in neat lines, to be checked off a register by our form tutors. I stood in my place, thinking to myself, I have done this, I have made the whole school stand out in the playground like dickheads for no reason at all. When we were dismissed and sent back to our lessons I wanted to say to the teacher, 'So, I have got no power and no influence over you or the class? Then why were you standing out in the playground?' I didn't say anything, but I knew who had had the last laugh.

During my years at Beacon School I set off the fire alarm on quite a few occasions. The mayhem this caused relieved the tedium and it was my way of getting back at the teachers who banished me from their classes. One such occasion was in fact a total accident, which someone from my class witnessed. I warned the boy not to grass on me or I would sort him out. Although it was truly accidental, I didn't go to the teacher and explain because I knew they wouldn't believe me. The idea caught on and at the end of term the alarms were always going off. I must admit that I was responsible for some of the incidents, but by no means all of them. It got so bad that at the end of the school year, on the last day of term, the fire alarms were turned off. That really spoilt our fun.

There weren't many fights at school and the few there were usually ended quite quickly because someone would break them up, more often than not a teacher. I did get into a few fights at school, mostly with sixth-formers and one or two people in my own year. I think the reason why I didn't get into too many fights was because of the people I went around with, one of whom was said to be the hardest boy in the school. I ranked about fourteenth hardest in the school, which was rather strange considering that the fights I was involved in were rare. At breaktime and lunchtime my friends and I would usually go to the same place. In one part of the school playground there were some tarmac tennis courts, one of which was frequented by the school rejects – smokers, truants, nutters and general drop-outs. This is where I would spend my break and lunchtime. In that part of the playground everyone knew everyone else. Quite a number of the regulars were kids from Pine Wood and Highbroom. There was a friendly atmosphere in our area except when, now and again, outsiders tried to come in and take over. Then things could get heated. But generally our part of the playground was a good place to be because nobody looked down on you if you were in care, in the bottom class, or in trouble.

Smoking was not allowed at school, of course, and I lost count of the times I was caught smoking. One such occasion was after school by one of the entrances. A teacher who didn't know me caught me smoking and asked me my name. I said, 'Fred Fever.' The teacher thought I was lying and asked me again what my name was. 'Fred Fever,' I repeated. In the end I told him to go and ask my head of house who I was. Then I walked out of the gate and didn't hear any more about it.

My friends and I would smoke at lunchtime and at breaktime when we had cigarettes. It was very difficult for the teachers to catch us as there were always quite a few of us, which made it hard to know who was smoking and who wasn't. Also, we would share a cigarette between us.

At Highbroom the staff were very strict as regards school attendance. They even made us go to school when we were ill. The staff were of the belief that if you said you were ill you were just trying to get a day off school. They didn't seem to consider it possible that you could ever really be ill. I personally found that attitude ridiculous, for although I hated school I hated being at Highbroom even more, and it was highly unlikely that I would pretend to be ill to stay at Highbroom rather than go to school.

Once the home sent me to school with a streaming cold, possibly flu, and I was sent back home by a teacher. It was often said among us children at Highbroom that 'they', the staff, would make you walk to school even if you had a broken leg. The staff's attitude seems even more perverse when I consider it more thoroughly. No one seemed bothered about what you did at school or whether you achieved good results, all you had to do was simply go there. So it would appear that the staff just wanted to get us off their hands for a few hours and were keener to shift responsibility for us than to show a genuine concern about our education.

Throughout my time at Highbroom I witnessed and experienced a great deal of staff violence. Ninety-nine percent of the violent attacks on the children were carried out by the male staff, although Mrs Jenton was known to lash out occasionally. The staff saw it as a means of control and punishment, but in fact it was blatant aggression and violence. One of the male members of staff had an uncontrollable temper, so whenever he lost his composure he would fly into a rage and hit any child in sight. In general the sort of violence I experienced was being slapped about and punched, usually in the head, legs and buttocks. Before, during and after an assault you would more often than not be pushed around, sometimes into walls or sharp objects. Often we were beaten with objects, such as rulers, pieces of wood or a belt. Obviously every child hates being hit, but we, as children in care, felt an added resentment because the staff weren't our parents and had no right to hit us. Many of the children who had parents threatened to get their mums and dads up to the house to sort the staff out, but throughout my years at Highbroom I never saw this threat carried out.

One evening in the dormitory, the lights went out while I was still reading. I said: 'I want to put my book away' in a silly, funny voice. Simon, a member of staff, came back down the corridor, flung open the door and threw me out of bed on to the floor. I was completely taken by surprise and the wind was knocked out of me. I lay on the floor thinking, What the fuck is going on? All I said was, I want to put my book away. Seconds later, with me still lying on the floor, Tony Mason came up the corridor and shouted at Simon. 'You leave him alone or I'll knock you out!' Simon went off and spoke to Tony and I was left alone. I got back into bed and never heard any more about the incident.

On another occasion Gary, Tim and I were talking in the dormitory around eleven-thirty when Mr Jenton burst into the room. He went straight over to Gary and started hitting him and shouting at us. I jumped out of bed before he could hit me and ran as fast as I could to the stairs. I jumped down them, about three or four at a time. I got to the bottom in record time, ran to the main front door and grabbed the handle. I stopped for a second and looked down at myself, standing barefoot and wearing only pyjamas. I wanted to open the door and run, run as fast as I could away from the living hell of Highbroom, but I knew it was no good running away. I would get nowhere dressed like that. I could go nowhere. I just stood there by the door waiting for the inevitable violence.

By this time Mr Jenton was at the bottom of the stairs and walking towards me. 'You're bloody mental, Fever!' He slapped me across the face. The slap hurt, but it was what he said that really concerned me. Jenton calling me mental. The bastard. If anyone was mental it was him, not me.

Being called mental really made me think hard. I was full of anger and resentment, that bullying bastard saying I was mental. If I was insane it was because of the way they ill treated and abused me at Highbroom. It was enough to drive anyone mental.

The physical pain of the beatings I could take, although it did hurt a great deal. Worse was the mental anguish which they brought. I felt trapped and totally helpless and defenceless. I knew that if I hit them back I would just get an even worse beating. The staff had all the power and they undoubtedly abused that power: they controlled the amount of food we had, the amount of sleep we had and the amount of money we had. They were in an awesomely powerful position and the beatings reinforced this. Yet their position didn't need further reinforcement. The status quo was perfectly clear to all of us. Whenever I took a beating from a member of staff I would see them for what they were; mindless, vindictive bullies who enjoyed picking on defenceless children. I always said to myself that one day I would get these bastards back. Yet, in hindsight, one can never totally redress the balance. Even if I was to get each and every member of staff who beat me and give them a good hiding things would not be equal. They are adults, I was a child, and they left me with psychological scars that may never fully heal.

During my years at Highbroom I ran away at least twice and I think there was a third occasion, but strangely I cannot remember any details of that. Children absconding from Highbroom was a very regular event. When there wasn't anyone on the run there was someone planning a bunk or at least thinking about it. Not a month went by without someone doing a runner or trying one.

Sometimes the children were on the run for only a few hours but there were once two brothers who stayed on the run for over a year, although they did have their father with them. Some of the parents actively encouraged their children to run away, but the prime reason for children running away, in almost all cases, was the way they were treated by the staff. It was often said that if you got away for forty-eight hours you had made it. Unfortunately, the average period of freedom was twenty-four hours.

In this day and age running away from a children's home is called 'voting with your feet'. The actions of myself and many others who lived at Highbroom was a loud, clear vote of no confidence. I am quite sure that very few of the incidences of running away or attempts to run away were written down in the day book. If all the attempts had been recorded then I am sure Barnardo's would have had an enquiry into why so many children were absconding from one of their institutions.

My social worker, Jim Johnson, made regular visits to see me at Highbroom. During the visits I didn't say very much to him.

He was responsible for me being at Highbroom in the first place, and what was more, he seemed to be on friendly terms with Mr Jenton. I had long since lost faith in Jim. I knew that telling him what went on in the home wouldn't guarantee my immediate removal. I would be left there, and what was certain was that staff would be ready to take revenge on me for what I had told my social worker. I was in a no-win situation. If I talked to my social worker and he didn't get me out my life would be even more miserable.

The chances of me being moved merely because I wanted to were non-existent. If 'they' decided to move you then you were moved – either way you had no say. The only good thing about my social worker's visits was that when he came the staff had to treat me decently for the duration of the visit, but things returned to normal the second the door closed behind him.

In spite of my lack of faith in Jim I was shocked when I learned in 1978 that he was leaving Barnardo's. I had known him for many years, and I didn't relish the prospect of getting to know a new social worker, who might well be a great deal worse. Jim's replacement, Denis Mead, seemed to me to be a very placid man and not at all assertive. After he had visited me twice I could tell that he was well in with Mr Jenton and would take his word rather than mine. As time went by and I got to know Denis Mead I realised that he was somewhat intimidated by Mr Jenton and would go along with anything he said. I was in no doubt that he would have been incapable of sticking up for me against Mr Jenton and the cruel system I lived under at Highbroom. After seeing what my new social worker was like I realised that the whole set-up was rotten and I had no way of escaping. When Denis came to see me I hardly ever said anything to him. I could see absolutely no point in talking to him – he was just another part of the horrible set-up. I never really trusted him. Anyone who could be friends with Mr Jenton was no friend of mine.

When you reached you fourteenth birthday at Highbroom you were given the choice of whether or not to go to church. If you chose to carry on everything stayed the same, but if you chose not to go, then you were forced to work. Virtually everyone who was fourteen no longer went to church – because they hated going, not because they wanted to work. I gave up as soon as I was allowed to. Some of us would have to work outside doing jobs such as gardening, sweeping the drive or working on the vegetable patch. Others worked in the kitchen, peeling and washing vegetables or doing the washing-up. Nobody enjoyed the Sunday tasks, but working outside, whatever the weather, was still preferable to going to church, and better than working in a horrible hot kitchen, with staff watching you all the time and shouting at you. I never understood why we had to work on a Sunday, considering that the staff were so religious. At church we had always been told that Sunday was a day of rest.

At school I had realised for a long time that other pupils were treated a lot less favourably than the sixth-formers. One day I decided to get a group of kids together and go down to the sixth-form building and take it over. I walked around the playground, drumming up other kids to join in the demo for equal rights with sixth-formers. It wasn't long before streams of kids started joining in just for the fun of it, not really knowing what it was all about. Before we reached the sixth-form building our numbers had swelled to about two or three hundred. We arrived to find all the doors locked and the sixth-formers inside shitting themselves. We called for them to come out and face us but nothing happened. A few minutes later the head sixth-form teacher came out and spoke to us. He was shouted down and heckled. Nothing came of our protest but it gave the teachers and sixth-formers something to think about.

During that lunchtime some windows were smashed and a few sixth-formers were beaten up. Later, a head teacher came up to me when I was on my own, and asked if I knew who had started the riot. I denied any knowledge of it but told him that if I heard anything I would tell him. I am sure he knew it was me, but he had no proof.

Mr Jenton was an active member of the local Rotary Club and knew a lot of other members socially. One was a keen Brighton and Hove Albion supporter who went to most of Brighton's home matches. This man wanted to take one of us from Highbroom to football matches when he went. For some reason I was the one chosen by Mr Jenton to go with him to watch football.

I was never really a Brighton supporter. The team I would have liked to have watched was Liverpool, my favourite team. But as that was impossible I often went to Brighton with the man from the Rotary Club. He would pick me up from Highbroom and drive me back after the match. I liked going to football – it got me out of Highbroom and Crowborough, and I was able to keep out of trouble. After a while, though, I stopped going because the man from the Rotary Club moved away and was unable to give me a lift.

During one school holiday I was introduced to a man from Barnardo's head office called Bernard Hill. He seemed a genuine person and keen to do his job well. After talking with the staff he came round and spoke to all the children individually, which was quite unusual. Although I didn't say a great deal to him at the time I remembered him saying I should let him know if I thought he could help me in any way.

After Bernard Hill had gone that day, I sat and thought about all the things I would have liked to have discussed with him on the subject of Highbroom. Then I thought, well, he's part of the system; he was probably just saying those things to keep us happy. I wanted to tell Bernard Hill about all the punishments, about the staff violence, about how many children ran away and how much I hated living there. But the more thought I gave to the matter the more it became clear that it would merely look like the complaints of one dissatisfied child who had been in trouble with the police and whose words had no real credibility. But a few weeks later I thought of a way to approach Bernard Hill. The children were fined when they did something wrong. As time went on more and more fines came into force. You could be fined anything from 5p to 50p for various supposed wrongdoings: eating bubble gum, swearing, smoking, being late in, wetting the bed, messing about and being late for school. The bigger crimes incurred larger fines. We asked where all the fine money went, and as usual were told that it was sent to underprivileged children in Africa. I was under no illusions: I was sure our money ended up in the staff's pockets. I loathed the fines, the dirty bastards nicking pocket-money from children in care. As more and more fines were brought in my pocket-money dwindled away to virtually nothing, as did many of the other children's. I knew that fining us was well out of order and I was determined to do something about it – after all, members of the general public had donated the money to children in Dr Barnardo's care, not to underprivileged children in Africa or for the staff to put in their pockets. I would write to Bernard Hill and tell him about the ridiculous and unfair fines imposed on the children by the staff.

The first thing I did when I thought of writing to Bernard Hill was to consult the other children. They all agreed that they hated the fines and wanted them stopped. If it came to it they would back me up. I asked Gary to write the letter. I dictated it, but I couldn't spell and had awful handwriting and thought Gary's effort would look better. I knew what to say, though. We both signed the letter and posted it to Barnardo's head office. I would have said more about what went on at Highbroom had I been able to count on the other children to back up my complaints. Without that I knew it would be my word against that of the staff, and I knew some of the children would be wary of getting involved.

Gary and I didn't expect much to materialise from our letter – except perhaps a bollocking from old man Jenton. However, a month or so later Bernard Hill came down to Highbroom and put an end to the fines. I was amazed. This bloke from head office wasn't a bullshitter, he really did mean what he said. That day he spoke to me briefly. He thanked me for my letter and told me that the fines had been stopped and wouldn't happen again. I thanked Bernard Hill for his help, for me and on behalf of the other children. They were all overjoyed that the fines had been stopped. Gary and I saw it as a great victory.

One afternoon I got into an argument with a female member of staff called Jackie. I cannot recollect what the argument was about but I think it had something to do with my behaviour. The argument got quite heated and I said to her: 'It's all right for you sitting there saying that, you can go home for weekends! I can't. You chose to come here, I didn't. You can leave this place, I can't!'

Then I walked out of the room leaving Jackie, a member of staff, in tears. Later, Jackie apologised for what she had said to me earlier. I didn't apologise for reducing her to tears. I didn't apologise because I meant what I said to her in the argument. I felt sorry that I had reduced her to tears, for she was a caring person, but what I said still stood. In hindsight I should have vented my anger at the other members of staff who were less caring.

From about the age of thirteen I worked part-time on nearby farms. I worked an average of four to five hours a week, usually on Saturday mornings and occasionally in the afternoon. I did various jobs, from bringing in hay to clearing out cowsheds, all unskilled and very hard work. The pay varied a little from farm to farm, but mostly I was on £1 per hour. I can't say I enjoyed the work, but the extra cash came in handy – I was used to labouring for nothing at Highbroom. I also did some gardening. There were many large, gracious houses around Highbroom, all of which had big gardens. Some of them were owned by very rich and powerful people. I much preferred the gardening jobs to farm work. The pay was the same but the work was more pleasant and less strenuous: sweeping up leaves, mowing lawns and generally tidying up garden debris. I even quite enjoyed gardening – you could see an immediate result from your work. Also, the people I worked for were often quite nice.

One of them was a managing director of Trebor. I got the job gardening for him through one of the boys at Highbroom – he needed someone to help him and I volunteered. When the boy left the home I took over his job. The couple, Mr and Mrs

Hamilton, were very kind and paid me more than I usually earned. They were fairly close to retirement, but even if their hair was going grey, they weren't old in their approach to life. Mr and Mrs Hamilton were very likeable, for they could show compassion and generosity. When it was time for a tea break they would invite me into the house and I sat with them, drinking tea and eating biscuits. I would chat to them and they often asked me questions about my family and my past. I didn't mind talking to them, because they talked to me about their lives. It was a proper conversation, not a one-sided interrogation, as most of my communications with adults were. One Saturday, as I sat and drank tea with them, they asked me if I would like to go on a week's holiday with them in Suffolk. Me? Go on holiday with them? At first I was too shocked to give them an answer. When I recovered it was all I could do to whisper my thanks and say that I would like that very much.

It was all arranged with the home, and my adventure started with a train journey from Crowborough to London, where I was met by the Hamiltons' grown-up daughter. I was not very familiar with the big city, so she travelled with me on the tube across London to Liverpool Street Station. I remember that it was a hot, sunny day. When we emerged at the train station from the underground, the heat hit us. The daughter sorted out my ticket, and I remember that she bought us both an ice-cream, because it seemed to taste especially good; the thick, creamy taste mingling with my excited anticipation of a real holiday with someone unconnected with the home. She saw me off on the train, and I was again on my own, travelling through the countryside on a hot, noisy train. It was packed with families bound for Clacton: the constant high-decibel excitement of the children was punctuated by an adult's sharp reprimand or the piercing wail of a baby as the train lurched chaotically through the Essex countryside. I didn't care.

At the station it made me happy to see anxious faces, actually looking for *me,* relax into relieved smiles as I appeared. Then we drove to the Hamiltons' holiday home.

The house had a thatched roof and was comfortable and

spacious. The setting was idyllic: it was surrounded by fields and countryside, and the nearest town was a few miles away. I spent a blissfully happy week in Suffolk. We went out for day trips, visiting other towns and places of interest. I was enchanted by it all – Mr and Mrs Hamilton had obviously thought carefully about what I might like to do or see. More importantly, throughout the week they treated me like one of the family – and I didn't even have to do any gardening!

As ever, though, my brief episodes of happiness had a price. As the week drew all too quickly to a close, the thought of what I had to go back to depressed me – somehow it all seemed so much worse when I had spent a week away from the home. I was extremely unhappy. I didn't want my holiday to end, I didn't want to go back to Crowborough and Highbroom. I returned with the Hamiltons by car, making one stop in London on the way to Crowborough. I had had a really smashing time and was very grateful to them for giving me such a nice holiday – it was one of the highlights of my childhood.

In 1978 I was introduced to a married couple called Mr and Mrs Shaw. I had been told that they wanted to look around Highbroom and that I was to show them around. I had no idea at the time that the couple were my prospective 'social contacts' – at my age further fostering was unlikely – and that they were in fact viewing me, not the home. As I showed them round they asked me questions about myself and Highbroom. The Shaws must have been reasonably satisfied with what they found because afterwards they agreed to be my social contacts, and at that point I was told exactly who they were and what they had been there for. The idea was that the Shaws would have me to stay at their house for intermittent weekends and parts of school holidays. In effect they would act as my parents when I was with them. I didn't take much persuading to accept this opportunity – a chance to get out of Highbroom and Crowborough now and again couldn't be passed by.

Philip Shaw was in his early fifties and was self-employed. He had a small shop with a sub-post office. He had himself spent nearly all his early life in the care of Dr Barnardo's before going into the armed forces, where he learnt his trade as a baker. Philip was working as a baker when he met Jane, and soon after they were married they bought a small shop, with some financial help from Jane's father. In their early days together Jane had worked in a telephone exchange as an operator, and by the time I was introduced to her she was in quite a good position at the GPO (now British Telecom). She was then in her early forties and in her spare time helped as a fund-raiser for Dr Barnardo's.

Because Philip had been brought up in Dr Barnardo's they both had a keen interest in the organisation. They had originally approached Barnardo's in the hope of either adopting or fostering a child. However, in order to satisfy Barnardo's vetting procedure, Philip needed to talk through his own childhood in care, and this he felt unable to do. Because he was not able to satisfy Barnardo's in this respect, the Shaws weren't recommended as potential adoptive or foster parents.

But Barnardo's didn't want to dismiss the caring married couple outright, and so they suggested the 'social contact' scheme, in which the Shaws would try to befriend a young person in care. I have absolutely no idea why I was chosen to be that young person. I didn't even know that such a plan was afoot until the whole thing was explained to me after I met the Shaws, nor did I know what having a social contact involved. I suppose I was one of the few children with no opportunity to spend holidays with their natural parents, and perhaps the powers that be at Highbroom took note of the success of my Suffolk holiday.

Whatever the reasons, very soon after being introduced to Mr and Mrs Shaw I went to stay at their home in Crawley for a weekend. I already had a vague idea of what their house looked like because Jane and Philip had told me lots about their home, pets and shop. But when we arrived at their house I was unprepared for how posh it was and how neat and tidy everything was. I couldn't understand why these people wanted me to stay in their house; I felt very out of place, as if my presence lowered the tone. The whole house, even the bathroom, seemed too grand for the likes of me. Two details which have always stuck in my mind were a small fish pond in the enclosed patio, and the drinks cabinet, which was in the shape of a boat. I was scared to touch anything in case it broke or got messed up. It took many weekends before I could relax even just a little bit. As Jane and Philip had no children, I had a bedroom of my own. It wasn't that big but it was warm and clean. The bed didn't have sheets and blankets – it had a duvet, which took some getting used to. It kept coming off in the night.

As the weekends went by I slowly got used to going to Jane and Philip's for the weekend. I went only one weekend in three. I looked forward to the visits, though, and wished that I could go there every weekend to get away from Crowborough. On the Friday night I would rush home from school and quickly get ready to go. Jane picked me up at around four-thirty. We chatted all the way to Crawley, where we picked up Philip from the shop and went on to the chip shop. Jane would buy me extra chips because she knew that I would be ravenous.

As time went on it became clear that I got on better with Jane than I did with Philip. I was able to communicate with Jane and we had quite long conversations. Although on the face of it Philip and I had a lot in common because of our similar backgrounds, we didn't in fact have much to say to each other. He was very much an introvert, and of course there was a big gap between our ages. Also I instinctively distrusted men: the cruelty and abuse I'd suffered in the past had been perpetrated by men, whereas the women in my life had, on the whole, been either caring or indifferent.

Some weekends I would take some school work to Jane and Philip's and they tried to help and encourage me. I only took work I thought interesting or I enjoyed because I rarely did any homework. On Saturdays I would go shopping with Jane and have a look around the town and sometimes buy a record. The meals at Jane and Philip's were out of this world. I had never before tasted such wonderful food. I really looked forward to mealtimes at the Shaws' – it was a real education for my taste buds. I was also allowed to drink alcohol, in moderation. We nearly always had wine with our meals. Another luxury was coffee, which was prohibited at Highbroom because it was too expensive. One thing was the same, though: when I went to bed on Saturday night I would already be thinking, tonight is my last night here, I will be in bed at Highbroom this time tomorrow. The thought of going back to Crowborough and Highbroom really overshadowed my Sundays at the Shaws'. But although I suffered from anxiety about going back, I tried my utmost not to show it. If Jane and Philip noticed that I was reluctant to go back they might have thought it best not to put me through that stress, and might have ended my weekends at their house. I certainly didn't want that to happen.

Some Sundays I would go out with Philip when he played golf with his friends. I wasn't that keen but I tried to show a little interest because I wanted to please the Shaws. I did give the golf a bit of a go, but I only succeeded in messing up the green, and the ball barely moved. However, now and again we went to a golf range where you could practise teeing off. I enjoyed that, it was quite good fun. The best part of the day out playing golf was the end, because then we would usually go into the clubhouse for a couple of beers.

I never could fully enjoy Sundays and tea that evening as it always seemed like my last meal in civilised society before it was back to prison rations. It felt like the condemned man's final meal. Often I dragged my heels getting ready and packing my things to go back. But I knew it made little difference – in a couple of hours I would be banged up at Highbroom. During the journey back to Crowborough I would get a sick feeling in my stomach and it got worse the nearer we got to Highbroom.

Back at the home life was much the same. One Sunday afternoon myself and a couple of friends from Highbroom were hanging around with two of our mates. We had little or no money and were generally bored. Then one of our friends from outside suggested we went glue sniffing. Nobody made any objections. I was about fourteen and had never tried glue before, so I decided to give it a go. I am not sure if any of the others had done it before but certainly for the majority of us it was the first time. One of the boys went home and got the glue and some bags. We were all set for getting out of our heads.

First we found a suitable location where we couldn't be seen and would be left alone. Then we all got down to some serious glue sniffing. I sniffed and sniffed for ages. The process of sniffing glue I didn't find enjoyable, but I persisted, sniffing away for all I was worth – I was anticipating a monstrous sensation of getting well out of my head. But all I ended up with was a horrendous headache. Some of the others seemed to be completely stoned and were behaving very stupidly and talking nonsense. Most of my friends seemed to be getting something out of glue sniffing, but I told them that I thought glue sniffing was a load of shit and that it didn't get me out of my head. I didn't want to do it again – I would stick to alcohol.

# 14
# Sexual Assaults

In the summer of 1978 I was walking alone along a country lane near Highbroom when a man pulled up in a van and asked if I would like a lift. I had never seen the man before, I didn't know him and I certainly wasn't going to get into his van. He asked me a second time if I wanted a lift as he was going the same way. I insisted that I would walk. After that he drove off. I was quite frightened by the experience and was relieved when he left me alone. I thought it was an isolated incident and that I had seen the last of the man. But a few days later I saw him again, and again he asked me if I wanted a lift. Again I said no. This time, however, he tried to strike up a conversation. I walked away from the van but he drove up alongside me and started talking to me. By this stage I was very frightened. I wasn't sure what he might do next. Eventually he drove off, after offering me money and cigarettes, both of which I refused.

The man went by the name of Billy Bulldog. He was short, squat, fairly broad, which was how, I imagine, he got his nickname. I also suspected that Billy had a vicious and violent side to him, as do some bulldogs. After he harassed me for the second time I became frightened, for it was quite clear that he wasn't going to go away. At this stage he hadn't made it clear what it was he wanted, beyond getting me into the van, but I sensed that he wasn't just offering me a lift, and that he wanted me in the van for another reason.

Throughout that summer I was constantly harassed by Billy

Bulldog. Week in and week out he would appear, asking me, did I want a lift? Did I want some money? Did I want a cigarette? Every time I said no to whatever he offered me. It must have been quite clear to him that I didn't want to take a lift or anything else from him; that I was scared of him and intimidated by him. Billy would always approach me when I was alone. I had by now a long-standing fear and mistrust of all men, especially middle-aged men. Over the years I had been subjected to a great deal of physical, emotional and sexual abuse by men, and their sheer presence was enough to make me feel uneasy. The quiet and secluded country lanes served only to heighten my feelings of fear and danger. Anyone who has been in a similar situation will understand that to be approached in such an environment by an intimidating man in a vehicle is very frightening. Billy ignored my refusals and pursued me relentlessly. It was as if the more I said no the more he harassed me. Unfortunately I had no alternative but to walk the long and winding country lanes. There were no buses which came anywhere near the home.

As I mentioned earlier, because of Highbroom's isolated location the children had to walk everywhere. The school was a two-mile walk; the town centre was a little bit further than the school. Even the nearest shops were about ten minutes' walk from the home. So, from the early summer of 1978, apart from my brief periods of sanctuary at the Shaws', I had no respite from persecution by somebody or other every hour of the day. At school I would be in trouble with the teaching staff and thrown out of classes; on my way home from school I would regularly be hounded by Billy Bulldog in the van. When I got back to the home the staff would give me a hard time by physically or emotionally abusing me, and often both. The abuse sometimes would go on into the evening, for example, when I was put on punishment. Then would come the peeling of tons of potatoes, or staring at walls, both of which would last for some time. Before the punishments even started, Mr Jenton would tell me off and physically assault me. Even when I was not punished or otherwise abused I would often have nightmares. So I lived with different forms of abuse twenty-four hours of the day.

I thought about telling the staff at Highbroom about Billy Bulldog. But, at the end of the day, I didn't trust them much more than I did him. The Shaws seemed – I don't know, just too remote from the reality of my life away from them. I didn't know what to do except hope and pray that he would leave me alone. I felt vulnerable, frightened and desperate. I had no one to turn to, nowhere to run. The people in positions of authority, power and trust had all, one by one, abused my trust. I was getting more and more frightened as the weeks went on. I thought that if I kept on saying no, one day he would get angry and attack me, kill me, even.

The pressure of Billy Bulldog's ever-increasing harassment became a terrible ordeal. I was now at breaking-point. I was literally frightened for my life. I had just started my fourth-year studies at school, and the next two years were the important years in which you were supposed to work hard for your final exams.

In early September I was working one Saturday in a garden which belonged to a wealthy company director who employed me on a casual basis. I worked there as and when I was needed. The grounds of the house were huge – too big for one family – and unbeknown to me the owner rented out part of the grounds to Billy Bulldog. Billy kept two ponies and his cart there. There were a couple of sheds which Billy used for housing the ponies and cart, and tools and straw. Totally unaware of this, I was working away in the garden when I saw Billy come up the drive in his van. My first reaction was one of shock, then horror. It was like a bad dream. What on earth could he possibly be doing here? He parked his van and then came over and started talking to me. My heart sank to the pit of my stomach and I felt sick. He explained about renting the space and asked me what I was doing there. Then he asked me to go over and see him later where the ponies were.

I was very frightened. I had been subjected to this continual pressure for so long that I had been worn down by him. My nerves were in complete shreds. I decided to go over and see him. I was shitting myself but I thought that if I didn't do what he asked now, another day he might try to kill me. I couldn't take any more of his harassment and desperately wanted him to leave me alone. I thought if I am still alive afterwards, at least he will stop hounding me and leave me alone. I gathered up all my courage and walked over to the sheds. The closer I got the more uneasy I felt. My pace got slower but somehow I arrived. Billy talked to me in a desultory way about the ponies. Then he opened the door and told me to go into the shed. I just knew that something awful was about to happen.

Billy could see the look on my face, he knew that I was shitting myself. He told me not to worry – he would pay me more money than I got for gardening. Then he told me to face the door and look through the small window and tell him if anyone was walking towards the shed. I looked through. There was no one in sight. I was frozen to the ground as I felt Billy move closer towards me.

He got down in front of me and undid my flies. He put his hand in my pants and took hold of my penis. Then he sucked my penis for some time. While this was going on I stared out through the small window. Even my eyes were paralysed. Although I could see through the window, life and time stood still. This was my first experience of oral sexual abuse and it was disgusting and terrifying. I felt as if I were dying, but at the same time apart, watching my own death, and powerless to prevent it. I was simply paralysed with fear. I tried to shout stop, stop, but when I tried to speak nothing came out. Eventually Billy stopped sucking my penis and did up my trousers. Then he gave me £5 and told me not to tell anyone.

I quickly left the shed and went back to work. I suppose I must have been in the shed for about ten minutes, but while it was happening it seemed like forever. I wasn't due to finish working until lunchtime, so I had to carry on gardening, right across from the shed, as if nothing had happened. When one o'clock came I rushed out of the place and across the road to

Highbroom. I told the staff that I had got really dirty doing the gardening and needed a bath.

In the bath I scrubbed and scrubbed, using tons of soap. I desperately tried to cleanse myself. No matter how much bathing and scrubbing I did, I still felt filthy dirty. The full horror of what had happened was sinking in. Billy Bulldog had sexually assaulted me. He had sucked my penis. I wanted to throw up. I hated myself. I thought I was disgusting and dirty. I couldn't stop thinking about what had happened and how dirty I was. I wondered if Billy Bulldog would leave me alone now.

I thought that he would – after all, he had got what he wanted. I felt very dirty and ashamed of myself; I hated myself. I considered myself the lowest form of life for having given in to that dirty pervert. I wanted to tell someone what had happened but, as with the harassment, I was frightened. More than that, I was too ashamed. I had a feeling that if I went to the police or the staff at Highbroom they would blame me and say it was my own fault. I was often blamed for things that weren't my fault.

I thought long and hard about who I could possibly tell, for I was going out of my mind and desperately wanted to talk to someone who could sort the matter out. The police were my first option, but I thought that they would blame me. I had terrible memories of the unexpected beating they had given me before and couldn't be sure they wouldn't do it again. As with Billy's earlier harassment of me, I just couldn't bring myself to trust the staff; also I felt that they didn't care about me anyway, so what was the point? I didn't even consider approaching my teachers at school. In most of their eyes I was nothing more than a troublemaker. Now that things had taken a more serious turn, I did consider telling Jane and Philip. Yet, in the end, I knew I just couldn't. I didn't really know them that well, and they didn't know what my life in care was really like. The staff had all been on best behaviour when they'd visited Highbroom, and I think they would have found it very hard to believe what really went on there. Jane and Philip's lives were so far removed from the life I was living. So it was impossible for me to discuss with them what was happening to me. I was certain Philip's life in Dr Barnardo's couldn't have been anything like mine. In last-ditch desperation, I thought about telling my mates at school. I soon abandoned that idea, because of the thought of being misunderstood and labelled as dirty, or a 'poof' or pervert.

I soon realised I could tell no one. I was in this alone, with no one to help me. The full enormity hit me: I could rely on nobody for help. I was at the mercy of all adults and those in authority. I had now been completely crushed by the system. I had no more fight to give, they had broken me. I had no power, no dignity, no pride, no self-respect. I had nothing more to give and they could take no more from me. They had already taken everything.

I was wrong about Billy Bulldog. The harassment didn't stop after his sexual assault. In fact, it intensified. By January 1979 I was being sexually abused on a regular basis, sometimes once or twice a week and sometimes more. The circumstances I was in – not being able to talk to or get help from anyone – put the abuser in a position of immense power.

As time went by I began to lose all hope and could see no end to the misery. My life was a living hell. I hated every hour of every day. Each day was a huge struggle from beginning to end. I seemed to be constantly in trouble. At school I couldn't concentrate and the teachers were always telling me off. On the way to and from school I was harassed by Billy Bulldog, and at Highbroom the staff would regularly hit and punish me. Over the years I had always fought back no matter what, but now I felt the fight seep out of me. All those years had taken their toll. I was fourteen and life had gone from bad to worse. My parents had been a great let-down, and I knew they could never save me from my desperate plight.

I had always fought back because I had always had hope of a better life. Having gone through so much and having seen no improvement I was now watching my life go down to the lowest depths imaginable, and I lost that hope. When I was in trouble at school, being punished at the home, or being sexually assaulted I was overcome by a sense of numbness. Only after the events had happened would I feel anger and loathing towards the adults who had committed these acts. After a while I felt nothing during or afterwards: not hope, not anger, not hatred, not happiness, not sadness, nothing. Emptiness. I was no longer alive. I was no longer capable of feeling. I was an object. I could see no way out, no hope, no future. I was emotionally dead.

Most of the sexual assaults were committed in Billy's car or van, usually in the evenings on my way home from school or late at night after I'd been out for the evening to a school disco, youth club or a friend's house, and also at weekends. He often gave me money after he had sexually assaulted me, usually a couple of pounds. I never thought that he paid me this money for sex, but rather to make him feel better. No amount of money would have been sufficient to pay for what he was doing to me. I didn't ask for the money but when it was given I took it. I didn't want it; I didn't want anything to do with him. I wanted to be left alone. I was not a prostitute, and this was not money for sex. It was sexual abuse of a very vulnerable teenage boy. I think Billy gave me the money to try and make me like him. It didn't work, of course. The fact that Billy gave me money made me feel even worse about myself, even dirtier.

I hated Billy for what he was, and what he was doing to me. The more the assaults took place the less I felt able to do anything about it. Billy became more and more demanding and kept on pressurising me to kiss him. I felt sick just thinking about it. I never gave in to him; I never, ever kissed him. For him to suck my penis was horrendous, but kiss him? No way. To kiss a person in my opinion is a sign of affection. I had no affection for the abuser, only hate. I loathed the bastard.

In the fourth year I was put into a non-exam maths class. In all other subjects I was at least taking CSEs. On my arrival I soon realised there was absolutely no point in doing any work or even doing as I was told. After all, for a long time the teachers had been using exams as the reason why you had to do the work. Take away the exam and you are left with no reason. From the outset I had no intention of doing one stroke of work in maths, I simply couldn't see any point in it. I still attended the classes, but all I did was mess around. I wasn't alone in this: at least six others in the class felt the same way as I did.

One day the maths teacher threw seven of us out of the class. We all went off for a smoke and then came back. The teacher then took all of us down to see the headmaster. From that day on the teacher refused to have me in his class. I was officially banned from my non-exam maths class, never to return. I spent the maths lesson with a girl who was also banned; together we would sit outside the headmaster's office and talk. We had no tutor and very little set work to do. For me it wasn't a punishment – it was preferable to the class by a long way – but of course I didn't learn any maths.

Not surprisingly, the disintegration of my life made my behaviour at school worse, and I was often sent to see the headmaster (or my head of house, or the deputy headmaster . . .) I think the teachers' intentions were to intimidate me, but this failed dismally. I couldn't care less which stern figurehead I went to see, and because I saw so many of them so many times it all became routine. I was never actually given the cane or suspended or expelled, but I was threatened with all of those punishments at one time or another. It made a change from standing outside a classroom.

I didn't bunk off school very often – not that I enjoyed school, but the name Fred Fever isn't exactly what you could call inconspicuous. My name probably jumped out of the register and hit the teacher on the nose. Furthermore, standing over six feet tall and having a very deep voice for my age, it was difficult for me to go physically unnoticed, either. And my erratic classroom behaviour hardly helped me to blend in.

Because of my notoriety it was very difficult for me to bunk off school without getting caught, so I was selective. Car maintenance was a lesson I would always skip. There were only two lessons a week, a double period every Thursday afternoon, and the teacher had a strange disposition. He clearly hated teaching. He would write loads and loads on the blackboard, which no one could keep up with, and which didn't seem to make sense. He would choose a couple of his favourite pupils and let them tinker with an old car while the rest of the class copied loads of shit off the board. He also had a bad temper and would throw heavy objects at anyone who stepped out of line. Because we took a dim view of him and his eccentric teaching methods a friend and I bunked off every lesson. Otherwise, I rarely played truant. Sometimes a friend might ask me to bunk off with him or her, so I would, as a favour, but it could be very boring away from school on your own.

Most of the time we would go into Crowborough and then off to some out-of-the-way place to lie low until school had finished. We passed the time talking, smoking and teasing one another, or ridiculing other people at school. Once two mates and I were bunking off at a girl's house. We got hungry and we made some spaghetti on toast. As we were halfway through eating it her father came home early and caught us. He was none too pleased to find us playing truant in his house and eating his food, and I think his daughter got it in the neck on that occasion. I liked bunking off school. It was good fun and an act of defiance against the system. It also provided a chance to get to know your friends better – there was plenty of time for long, one-to-one conversations without the need to impress anyone.

When I was in the fourth and fifth years I went to the school's discos on a Thursday night. The home allowed me to go as long as I got back by ten-thirty. I would meet up with my mates, and we always thought that tonight would be the night when we would get off with a girl. This was hardly ever the case. Sometimes we had a few lagers at the school disco, when money allowed. At nearly all school discos there was a fight, usually between two people, but now and again there was a gang fight, mostly mods versus rockers. I got into one or two fights at the school discos but I was never heavily involved.

One evening at the school disco I had a chance with a really pretty girl from the fifth year – a year older than me. I had been told that she fancied me and all I had to do was talk to her. I was really nervous but in the end I decided to give it a go. We talked for a while and danced a couple of times to slow records. Then it was ten o'clock, and the disco finished. The girl invited me home for coffee; I couldn't believe my luck. But then I remembered I had to get home or I would be in big trouble. I wanted desperately to go, but I was forced to decline, and left in a hurry to get back to Highbroom on time.

After that night I couldn't face her. I felt really awful – she must have thought that I didn't like her – the truth was that I didn't want to explain to her that I lived in a children's home and I was acutely embarrassed that I wasn't allowed to stay out late. I never spoke to her again.

On Wednesday nights I often went to the local youth club. It wasn't exactly great there but it meant you could get out of the home for a night. It was about fifteen minutes' walk and I had one or two friends there. The facilities weren't anything special. It had been run down for years, and so nobody treated it with any affection or respect. The atmosphere was not particularly enticing. Now and again they would stack the battered table tennis tables against the graffiti-covered walls, put away any unsquashed ping-pong balls and have a disco at the youth club. These nights were usually a disaster and invariably ended in a fight.

In March 1979 I wrote a letter to my mother and father suggesting the idea of spending my half-term with them. I thought it would be a good way of us getting to know one another, without either side making a major commitment. It was not a plan I particularly relished, and I knew the situation would not be easy to handle, but I thought it was for the best: after all, they were my real parents and I just had to get out of Highbroom, out of Crowborough and out of care. I tried to believe it could work out between my parents and me. I had to believe it could – it was my last chance. And yet, deep down, I knew all along there was no way it ever would.

I cannot recollect what else I put in the letter for it was many years ago. But I vividly remember every detail of the reply from my mother, for two reasons: the first due to its extraordinary content and the second because it is the only letter that I ever received from my mother or father. I was appalled at how blunt and unhelpful it was. I read it over and over again and thought about it a lot. I decided to ask my social worker if the two of us could go and speak to my parents about the letter and about me going to stay there for half-term. I have kept the letter from my mother safe for many years now. Here is a copy of that very letter.

Dear Fred

I am sorry that you can not come home like that. if you want to come home, ~~to send~~ I shall want you for good. I can not have you like you say. So let me know.

Love mum

A few days after I spoke to my social worker, arrangements were made for us to go and see my parents one evening after school. Denis Mead picked me up from the home. I hadn't eaten but I'd had just about enough time to change out of my school uniform. I was very apprehensive about going to see my mother and about how I would be able to handle the subject of the letter, but something had to be sorted out.

My social worker was quite used to getting letters like this from my mother, demanding my immediate return home. He told me that she had written to Barnardo's on many occasions with the same demand. During the journey we discussed the letter and its implications. I was in a real dilemma. I wanted desperately to get out of Highbroom but I didn't want to rush home to my parents for good just like that. I really didn't want to go home just for half-term, I needed to find out whether it would ever be possible for me to go and live with my parents permanently.

When we arrived at my parents' house in Kent, it was still light. We went up the path and knocked on the door. There was no answer. We knocked again, then waited a few minutes and knocked once more. No answer. Eventually we went and sat in the car, from which vantage-point we could keep an eye on the house. While we waited Denis told me that he had come to see my parents at other times and that they had pretended to be out when they were in. We had been sitting in the car for about fifteen minutes when Denis noticed a movement inside the house. We got out of the car and knocked on the door again. Still no answer. We knew my parents were in so we just carried on knocking. After a very long five minutes my father opened the door a crack, just enough to put his head round. He looked very upset and I think he was almost in tears. Denis and I asked if we could come in but my father said we couldn't. We said we had come to talk to them about the letter my mother had sent. My father then closed the door for a few minutes. When he reopened it again he told me that my mother didn't want to see me and didn't want to talk to me.

My heart sank like a stone. I wanted to cry and scream for my mother. I couldn't believe that she could reject me like that. I didn't know what to say or do. It was one of the saddest and most profoundly disturbing moments of my life. I had longed all my life to have a real mother and father and now here I was, standing on the front step of my parents' house, being totally rejected by my mother. I wanted to die there and then. I had kept myself going all those years by dreaming of the happy day when I would return to my loving parents. Even the discovery of what poor parents they were had not completely destroyed that dream, but now it was smashed into tiny fragments which poured from my heart. I could take being rejected by the rest of society, but not by my own mother.

I walked slowly down the path towards my social worker's car. I wanted to get away from there fast. Meanwhile, my father had come out of the house and was speaking to Denis. He said that he would like to let us in but he couldn't because of my mother. He then suggested to my social worker that we should go and see his sister, my auntie, who lived a few miles away in St Mary Cray, Orpington. My father assured Denis that we would get a warm welcome. In the car, Denis asked me if I would like to go and see my auntie. I was completely numb. I was in no mood for seeing anyone right then, least of all another relative. Denis seemed to think it might salvage something from the situation and talked me into it. Quite frankly I couldn't have given a toss who I went to see. Nothing mattered any more.

We had to make a couple of stops on the way to my aunt's house to ask directions, but it wasn't far. When we arrived I was past being nervous, past any feelings of anticipation whatsoever. I was in deep shock after what had happened at my parents' house. Denis knocked on the door, and my auntie answered the door within a minute or two. There stood this grey-haired woman who looked to be in her late fifties. Her clothes weren't posh but she was clean and tidy, and reassuringly ordinary. My social worker did all the talking, I just stood there feeling awkward and unwanted, not knowing quite what to say. My auntie invited us in. We went into the house and sat down in the front room, and she brought us a cup of tea. As we drank it, Denis Mead told my Aunt Dorothy all that had happened. I didn't say much but listened to the conversation intently. Aunt Dorothy was clearly overjoyed to see her long-lost nephew for the first time in fourteen years. She was upset about what had happened at my parents' house but was very pleased that we had come to see her.

My auntie's house was a small one-bedroomed bungalow, homely and warm. I was later to spend my half-term holiday at my auntie's house which I enjoyed very much. Because Auntie Dorothy was so much older than me there was quite a generation gap, and holding conversations with her was sometimes quite difficult. Although we were closely related, in effect we were total strangers. At first she seemed a little strange, but as I got to know her a little I realised that she was also a creature of habit, gentle, and quite shy. Auntie Dorothy had a cat she was very fond of; she likes animals a lot and is a vegetarian, and helps to raise funds for the RSPCA. At half-term I went up to London nearly every day with Aunt Dorothy and a distant relative. During the week's holiday we visited museums, art galleries, and various tourist sites in London. I haven't got any strong memories of these visits because I wasn't really interested and found them a bit boring. In the evenings, Dorothy and I would watch some television or, if it had been a tiring day, after a late tea we would have an early night. During the week I had to sleep on a camp bed in Dorothy's living-room. Throughout the week I tried to find out what I could about my family by asking her some questions, but I found it quite difficult, and I didn't want Dorothy to get annoyed with me for pestering her with lots of questions. I realised midway through the week that Dorothy just wanted to treat me well, and didn't feel that easy discussing the family with me. I didn't find it very relaxing being with my auntie, for it seemed very odd spending time with a relative having never lived at home. Although I didn't really know Dorothy, by the end of the week I had grown to like her. The visit ended with a kiss and a hug and also a promise to keep in touch.

After that first meeting my social worker drove me back to the home in Crowborough. I was pleased that I had met my Auntie Dorothy that evening, although I was hardly in a state to cope with it. She really seemed like a warm and caring person, and it was a grain of comfort. Yet the meeting in no way compensated for the rejection by my mother. More than anything in the world I wanted to be loved and accepted by both my parents. I was devastated by the rejection, and I have never fully recovered from it. I probably never shall. Although I did spend my half-term holiday at my aunt's that was the only and last contact I had with her for many, many years. She didn't keep in touch either by letters or phone calls, and I didn't keep in contact with her – I was very upset about my parents and found it difficult to have anything to do with my 'family'. I also had too many other problems on my mind, and all my thoughts and energies were taken up with just getting through each day.

After the traumatic episode at my parents' house, life at Highbroom deteriorated steadily. I discovered that I was only one of Billy Bulldog's victims. He sexually abused many young boys in the Crowborough area and by the summer of 1979 he was regularly assaulting several young boys from Dr Barnardo's at Highbroom. I was one of those boys. I cannot comment on what other victims' feelings were at the time, as sexual abuse can affect people in different ways. It would not be right for me to speculate about other children's horrendous experiences of sexual abuse, or to name or implicate them. At the time the abuser's conspiracy of silence condemned each of us to our own lonely misery.

When I found out that Billy was abusing other children from Highbroom I felt sick and angry. I hated Billy so much I wanted to kill him. Often at night I lay awake unable to sleep, and would think of ways of killing him. I would even act out the scene in my mind. I thought of getting a knife and stabbing him to death, or battering him with a heavy object, like a hammer, and visualised strangling him with a scarf, or a long piece of cloth.

I favoured strangulation because I felt the other means were very messy and unreliable. He might live after a stabbing or battering. Another thing that appealed to me about strangulation was watching Billy Bulldog suffer, fighting for breath, and finally watching him die. However, I never put my plan into action; I was far too frightened of Billy to do that. But the consequences of murder never entered my mind. All I wanted to do was kill the bastard.

One Saturday lunchtime in the autumn of 1979, I and some of the other children who were victims of sexual abuse were queuing up for our dinner. It just so happened that no other children were around at that moment. I was in the front of the queue, and went into the kitchen first to receive my lunch, closely followed by the others. Mrs Jenton looked up at us and said in a loud and threatening voice: 'I see we have a load of nancy boys in the home!'

I couldn't believe what I was hearing. Mrs Jenton calling us nancy boys. The staff *knew* that children in their care were being sexually abused by a pervert and were doing nothing about it, and even worse than doing nothing, were ridiculing us by calling us nancy boys? I was mortified. Until Mrs Jenton had said that I hadn't dreamt that the staff knew what was happening. My worst fears were now confirmed. The staff at Highbroom didn't give a shit what happened to the children. I was fifteen at the time and now, faced with the full horror of the knowledge that staff at Highbroom would actually stand by and let me and others be assaulted sexually by a paedophile, I knew with cold certainty that I would never get out of this systematic cycle of abuse while I remained in Crowborough.

At that stage in my life I am not sure who I hated most, the staff at Highbroom or Billy Bulldog. I knew the staff were bastards but this was too much to cope with. The fucking bastards knew and did nothing.

At Highbroom I failed to have any meaningful relationships with girls. At about the time when I started being sexually abused, friends of the same age were beginning to form relationships with the opposite sex. The fact that I was being regularly assaulted by a pervert meant that my adolescent years and experiences were of a different nature. For me this meant isolation from my friends. I would pretend to be coping and enjoying life, and never did I let on that I was in any way having a horrendous time. What was happening to me during my early teens implanted significant feelings about sex itself. I thought it was dirty, painful and disgusting, and failed to see where the enjoyment lay. My only experience of a sexual nature was abuse. I was unable to feel positive about having any form of close relationship with anyone. On the few occasions when I dated girls, it was a disaster. I didn't know how to act. The main problem I had was letting girlfriends get close to me. I didn't want them near me as I felt so dirty; I didn't want them to know anything about myself and my life in care. I was scared that if they got near to me, I would make them dirty too.

By then I couldn't feel love for anyone, no matter who they were. Many years of physical, emotional and sexual abuse had left me hollow, the shell of a person without anything inside. I had no long-term friendships, I never knew love and security, and in turn I was incapable of conveying love.

Yet because of Billy Bulldog I felt a desperate need to assert my heterosexual orientation. I wanted to have sex with a girl. I needed to do this in order to preserve my sanity, or so I thought, for I was going out of my mind. I was naturally attracted to girls, but I was confused about everything because all my sexual experiences so far had consisted of abuse by males. There was a girl called Sheila at Highbroom who was the same age as me. I didn't fancy her, but she was close at hand and seemed approachable. I decided to ask her if she would have sex with me. I had no intention of having a relationship with her, I just wanted to have sex.

One Sunday afternoon Sheila and I were alone in the grounds of Highbroom. I plucked up courage and walked over to her. There was no beating about the bush. I coldly asked her, 'Do you want to have sex with me?'

She said, 'No I don't,' and quickly walked away. Never again did I ask Sheila for sex. I didn't feel at the time what I said was wrong, but I was too embarrassed to try it again. At the age of fifteen I now had very distorted ideas about sex and sexual relationships. I saw sex as a cold act between two people and nothing more.

# 15

# Nobody Cares

In 1979 I spent my summer holidays at Jane and Philip's. I was pleased about going to stay with them, for it meant six weeks away from Highbroom and Crowborough, six weeks free from abuse. At the beginning I helped out in Philip's shop, serving the customers and stocking up. I quite enjoyed working there. It was a new experience for me. Although I wasn't great at adding up I managed to muddle through. However, Philip already employed two women in the shop so there wasn't a great deal to keep me occupied.

One day Philip got talking to one of his suppliers who ran a mushroom farm just outside Crawley. Philip asked the man whether he had any summer jobs at the farm. Philip put me forward as he knew I wanted a job for the summer. It was agreed that I would start the following Monday. Philip would drive me there early in the morning for an eight o'clock start.

The work was physically quite hard and mundane. I was employed along with four others to clean out the beds and sheds at the mushroom farm. It was blisteringly hot in the sheds and it was dirty work, and I would sweat buckets and go home filthy from head to foot. I can't say I enjoyed the work but it kept me busy, and earning my own money gave me a sense of freedom and autonomy. The wages were not that great – I earned about £40 a week – but by the time I finished working at the farm I had saved £160. For someone like me that was a lot of money.

In 1978 Jane and Philip had gone to Corfu for their holiday

and had promised me that this year they would take me abroad. I had never been on a foreign holiday and so I was looking forward to going, but in the end they decided on a camping holiday in Dorset, during the last week of my summer holiday. Throughout the week I was very conscious that it was my last week of freedom. I kept trying to block out of my mind the thought of going back to Crowborough and Highbroom. I enjoyed the holiday and I needed the rest after working at the mushroom farm, but as ever the spectre of Highbroom marred the last day.

When I arrived back at the home in Crowborough I felt totally alienated. I felt that this wasn't where I lived – my home was with Jane and Philip. I had now experienced a new way of living and the contrast hit me after such a long time away from institutional life.

In December 1979, after breaking up from school for the Christmas holidays, I again went to stay with Jane and Philip. I had been looking forward to the holiday for some time. Philip's shop was very busy at that time of year, so I helped out. On the last day of business before Christmas, Philip invited all his staff and their partners, plus me, to the local pub for a Christmas drink and a bite to eat.

There were eight of us in total: Clare, Morag and Mary, who worked for Philip, and their partners, Philip and myself. Although I was fifteen at the time, I wasn't brought into the conversation apart from being asked the odd dead-end question. So I sat to one side and drank, absorbing the conversation going on around me. I didn't mind that much for I was quite happy eating and drinking lager.

Suddenly the conversation changed from trivial matters to families and children. I listened intently, eager to hear what everyone had to say. Although we were all seated around the same table, I think the others had forgotten I was there. Clare, who was the mother of two teenage boys, said how wonderful bringing children into the world made her feel and how she enjoyed watching them grow into adults. Philip said that he didn't like the idea of children. You bring them into the world and then they come along and take all you have worked hard for. I couldn't believe I was hearing this from Philip, my social contact. I sat back and thought to myself, what the fuck am I doing here? Meanwhile Clare and the others began to shout Philip down, but he stuck to his own opinion. By this time I was trying to block out everyone in the pub. I didn't want to hear another word.

The rest of my Christmas holiday was clouded by what Philip had said in the pub. I thought of telling Jane, but decided against it. After all, she was his wife and I would probably be the loser. From then on I knew that deep down Philip didn't want me in his house, and although Jane may have genuinely wanted me there I no longer felt at ease with the situation.

At one point there was talk of me going to live with the Shaws permanently after I left school. Although I wasn't totally sure, it seemed to be the best available choice. It was either living with the Shaws or going to yet another institution. As time went on and my schooling was coming to a close, the Shaws became less and less enthusiastic about having me to live with them.

There were areas of worry on the Shaws' part. They felt I was apathetic and lacked motivation about the future and my career. They discussed the future with me and talked about me getting a job at Gatwick Airport while attending further education in the evenings. However, at the beginning of 1980 the Shaws started looking for a new house. By about March they had already decided to buy a derelict building which was part of an old disused convent in East Grinstead. They planned to make a temporary home in one part of the building while they worked on converting the rest of it into a beautiful house. The Shaws then broke the news that I couldn't go and live with them after all, citing the move as the principal reason.

When I learnt of this I was very upset. I had yet again been let down by adults who supposedly cared about me. On top of that, I knew that my future didn't look at all rosy now. I had thought it was all too good to be true, these posh people letting me come to live with them for good. I should have known by then that nothing good ever came from adults. My one and only hope of escaping institutions had now been obliterated. I faced a very uncertain future.

In the early months of 1980 I was taken to see the Barnardo's printing school by my social worker. I think the idea was to give me an option for when I left Highbroom. If I chose to go there it would solve two problems: first, where they were going to put me next, and second, it would give me a job. The visit was due to last a whole day and one night.

The first thing I didn't like about the place was its location. It was out in the countryside, miles from anywhere. I'd had enough of that at Highbroom. As soon as I walked into the printing school I felt uneasy; there was something about it that wasn't right. Every part of the school seemed dull and oppressive. I met some of the people who were training there, and none of them appeared happy with their lives. I instinctively knew it wasn't for me and the thought of being stuck there for the next few years made me shudder.

My social worker took me out for lunch, and I made two things very clear to him. One, I didn't like the place and didn't want to go there when I left school, and two, in no circumstances was I going to stay there overnight. Denis could see how strongly I felt about it so he didn't push the issue. In the afternoon I was due to look around the hostel accommodation as part of my tour, but because I had made a strong objection to the printing school, my social worker saw no point in wasting time there. However, I still had to have an interview with the person who ran the printing school. In the interests of saving time I laid my cards on the table straight away at that meeting. I said I didn't want to go there when I left school and therefore there was no point in staying the night. The interviewer didn't seem at all bothered, so obviously I wasn't the first person to turn down a place at the Barnardo's printing school. I felt so uneasy at the printing school that for once I wanted to get back to Highbroom. I don't know what it was about it – a terrifying glimpse of a grey half-existence that was my destiny, perhaps? – but it gave me the shivers.

Every six months when you are in care, the authorities have what is known as a review. A review is to assess how the child has progressed over the last six months and to see what needs to be done during the following six months. At Highbroom I was never once allowed to attend my six-monthly review. In the spring of 1980 I was allowed to attend what I thought was a review, but which turned out to be a case conference, a meeting usually held when major decisions about a child's future need to be taken at relatively short notice.

The people who attended the case conference were Mr Jenton and another member of staff from Highbroom, Denis Mead, Jane and Philip Shaw, my teachers from school and myself. For the majority of the meeting I sat and listened to what everyone had to say. I couldn't get over seeing two of my teachers at the home, discussing my life. I thought, this is ridiculous, as if my teachers or anyone else in the room gives a toss about what's going to happen to me. It was in this meeting that I was officially told that upon leaving school I would not be able to go and live with the Shaws because of their house move. In fact that was precisely why the case conference had been called. Now that I would not be going to live with the Shaws, what were they going to do with me? As usual there were not many options from which to choose. I could not go and live with Jane and Philip, I didn't want to go to the printing school, so that left only one alternative, a hostel.

At the time, Dr Barnardo's ran two hostels for young people aged sixteen plus. One of these was in Croydon, the other in Kingston-upon-Thames. It was suggested that I should go to the Kingston hostel as I knew a few people there. I asked the meeting whether there was any other choice apart from going to a hostel. My social worker said there wasn't. After further discussions it was decided that I should go to Kingston hostel for three weekends before finally deciding whether to move there permanently. Everyone at the conference seemed to be happy with the outcome – everyone, that is, except me. What decision was there to be made? What would happen if I refused my one option, the hostel? Although I had yet to visit Kingston, I felt sure that was where I would be sent after leaving school and that my weekend visits there were no more than a formality. My future had been decided by a group of people who basically wanted me out of the way, and they were satisfied that this had been achieved. The fact that I attended the case conference had no bearing on the outcome. My role at the meeting was that of an onlooker, not a participant; my opinion counted for nothing.

And so the end of my education at Beacon School was in sight. I have picked out a varied but revealing selection of comments from my school reports. The remarks made are from different years, for different subjects, and from different teachers.

'He still needs constant reassurance but responds well to encouragement and praise. He has an inferiority complex which restricts his natural ability of oral expression.'

'Fred started off well in the form but unfortunately he has just stopped working and now prefers to play around.'

'Speed of work is still Fred's weakness but he copes with this now. He retains information and is able to produce this in a written test. Second in the examination – well done.'

'Fred is capable of good work in class but his behaviour can often disrupt the class.'

'Fred deserves congratulations for the work he has put into this subject and in particular in the last unit of the course.'

'Fred has had to be withdrawn from regular mathematics lessons to work on his own, because of difficulties with his behaviour.'

'Fred badly lacks concentration. I find him to be untrustworthy and unable to sustain any real effort. He is content to chatter and do menial tasks and is likely to gain little from the course until his attitude matures.'

'Fred makes no effort at all in this subject and cannot expect to do well until he does.'

'Fred continually wastes his time in class. He cannot hope to achieve any sort of standard if he makes so little effort to get down to any sort of work.'

'Obviously a lot of hard work is needed. We would welcome some co-operation in seeing that he settles down to do his homework properly.'

After I left school I asked Denis Mead if I could have my old school reports from my file. He agreed and brought them on his next visit. Somehow there was a mix-up and what Denis actually brought were some unofficial school reports that I was never intended to see. These unofficial reports had been written yearly and sent direct to the home, and the authors remained anonymous. I kept them and asked Denis for my official school reports, which he later found and gave to me. Those unofficial school reports are reproduced on pages 193 to 195.

My first reaction to the unofficial reports was shock. I was astounded to read what my teachers secretly really thought of me, and how badly they judged me. But then I realised this was yet another example of the lack of any real communication between those supposedly looking after my welfare and education and myself. The unofficial reports, and my ordinary school reports for that matter, were yet another example of how adults in powerful positions were labelling me and writing me off.

When I lived in Crowborough there were very few, if any, job opportunities. If you had poor or no qualifications then the only job available in the Crowborough area was in Buxted chicken factory. The chicken factory was predicted for me – if I played my cards right. The teachers would constantly sneer that I would end up in a detention centre, borstal and prison. I hated these speculations. I had already spent a lifetime in institutions and didn't relish the idea that I would never be free from institutional life.

The teachers' continual prejudiced insinuations that I would be going to a detention centre, borstal and then prison didn't in any way change my behaviour or attitude towards people in authority, or towards the system itself. When they made these remarks I knew they were talking a load of shit and knew bugger all and it wouldn't be long before I proved them all wrong.

## SUBJECT REPORT - FRED FEVER

MATHS

Fred is very limited in this subject and lacks concentration. His progress, if any, is very slow and he soon loses interest.

ENGLISH

Fred's work has deteriorated this half year. His attitude has changed considerably from a boy keen to learn all he could to improve his standard of work, to one who has become lethargic and couldn't care less. His written work can be neat when he makes an effort but more often he becomes impatient with the exercise or task in hand. He has a good imagination and some experience from which to write interesting essays. His self control is now somewhat lacking; he takes offence easily and will refuse to work at all on some days if something or someone annoys him. One used to be able to persuade him to work well but he is becoming uncooperative and resistant to gentle discipline. He will become arrogant and downright rude on occasions when corrected, to draw class attention to himself.

HISTORY

Fred seems more able to cope. He doesn't get so frustrated if he is behind in his work. He has maintained his previous standard of work. He can retain information and does well in tests based on class work and home work.

SCIENCE

He has conceptual difficulties with the subject but keeps a keen interest, especially in discussion periods. In practicals he does sometimes need prompting to continue an experiment etc. Written work is poor, with little control. Behaviour generally good.

HOUSE COMMENT

Fred tries to give me the impression he is the innocent who is drawn into things by other 'evil' boys. I do not go along with this whole-heartedly. Fred is devious and does know what he is getting involved in. School work has been affected by recent events. It has been suggested to me that Fred should be in a special unit for devious, maladjusted children. I feel that there are probably more urgent cases than Fred in the area and there is no doubt a shortage of places.

## SUBJECT REPORT - FRED FEVER. 13.EVA

ENGLISH
In this group (3P) Fred performs reasonably well in English. His presentation is acceptable and it seems to be one of his better subjects. He has shown a surprising interest in poetry recently.

MATHS
Fred is making no progress in this subject. He has a long-established dislike for the subject and he refuses to try and overcome this.

P.S.C.E. (Personal, Social and Careers Education)
He is very pleasant and interested in P.S.C.E. In a recent test he took three times as long as the rest of the class but the result was quite good.

BIOLOGY
Fred always works well. His level of understanding is not particularly high but he is interested in the work and always contributes well to the lessons. His behaviour is normally good and overall I am very pleased with his progress. Written work lets him down and he finds it difficult to generate much enthusiasm.

PHYSICAL SCIENCE
Fred has continued to work hard throughout the year. He is still rather slow when it comes to writing but he is improving. He is a very likeable lad. He is making slow but steady progress - his determination will carry him through.

GEOGRAPHY
On the whole Fred works quite well and shows interest in the different lessons and countries we have studied recently.

R.E.
Cooperative, sensible behaviour - happy disposition - works on average level for 3P.

ART
Fred is easily distracted when working in this subject, but his work is reasonably satisfactory. His painting and composition work is progressing slowly, his drawing is still rather weak. His behaviour has improved and he has been very helpful in class.

## Interim Subject Report - Fred Fever. 14.EVA, 4R

ENGLISH

I have been impressed by Fred's enthusiasm for this subject over this past year. His essays show maturity and sensitivity which is coupled with a surprisingly large vocabulary. He is rather weak technically, but his ideas do counter this lack somewhat. I have a minor quibble over his homework. It is produced, but rarely on time. Fred knows his limitations but is prepared to work at them, to overcome any barriers. All in all, Fred seems to have had a good year - I hope that his fifth year will be equally successful.

MATHS

I find difficulty in writing anything which shows Fred in an advantageous light. He is extremely low in ability and consequently relies on others around him, i.e. copying. He has not shown any interest or ambition to do better or to stand on his own two feet. He is noisy, outspoken and has shown no intention to curb his occasional foul language. At this time he is spending his Maths lessons out of the room (with DHM) but is handing me no work to check - the intention (forlorn perhaps) is to make him change his ways. Time will tell.

COMMUNITY STUDIES

I am very pleased with Fred's work in this subject. His application to his work puts him ahead of some of his more intelligent colleagues.

INTEGRATED SCIENCE

Fred's work is erratic; he is difficult to motivate and interest. However, he is a very pleasant member of the set and he does on occasions produce work of a reasonable standard. His written work varies from very poor to being well presented. At the present time he is working on a project which, when complete, I believe will be of a good standard. Fred needs to concentrate and become more involved with all of his work since he would then achieve a reasonable result in this subject.

HOME AND LEISURE

Although Fred has no great aptitude for climbing (in fact he seems quite petrified!) I have to admire his determination and persistence, since he has achieved more than I would have thought possible after his first laboured efforts.

ART

Fred's work and his behaviour have both improved over the past months. He is fairly consistent in producing his homework.

P.E.

Fred has worked well without any problems, all year. He lacks coordination but has improved.

The teachers at Beacon School also said I would never pass any exams. I didn't want to take my CSE examinations because I knew long before leaving school that CSEs were not worth the paper they were written on. However, I decided to sit them purely to prove a point. I passed all my five CSE exams. I didn't exactly get brilliant grades, but I passed, which was the object of the exercise. Thus I showed that some teachers at Beacon School really talked a load of shit.

From the beginning of 1980, children started to leave Highbroom and weren't replaced. Highbroom, the house of horror, was finally going to be closed down. It was too late to do me any good but perhaps other children would be spared some of the terrors I'd endured. Many of the children who left at this time went home to live with their parents, while others were found foster parents, some of whom lived in the local community. I, however, wasn't to be fostered and neither was I going home to my parents. I was being sent to a hostel. As the months went by I watched a steady trickle of children go home to their families. I saw all my friends leave. At one stage there was only Sheila and me left. Then even Sheila left, and for the last two months of my time there, there was only me.

So except for the staff I was the only person at Highbroom, and had the big, cold, ugly mansion all to myself, the place I hated so much but yet would be the last to leave. I was pleased for the others who had left – they had got away, and that gave me some consolation during my isolation. I felt sure Mr Jenton had a hand in planning it. I felt like Rudolph Hess in Spandau, except that the only crime I'd committed was being born. Alone, the last prisoner, I waited for my release. Meanwhile, time passed slowly, and I rattled around in the dark house, with no one to talk to except one member of staff.

Mr Jenton and the staff had, over the years, put me through some awful punishments, but this was by far the worst – two months of psychological torture. I felt very insecure and even more vulnerable being there alone. There were no other children to offer comfort and solidarity – it was just me and them now. At times I didn't know if my nerves could stand it, but I managed to hang in there to the end. The worst thing about watching others leave to go home was knowing that that day would never be mine. I could never go home. I had no home.

A week or so before I was due to leave Highbroom, Billy Bulldog sexually assaulted me. At least, I thought to myself, this will be the last time. I have seen the last of him. But there were still some days to go before my departure and unfortunately they proved to be too many. I was sexually assaulted only two days before leaving Crowborough. This last assault was one of the worst to bear because I had been sure that the previous one would be the last. I didn't expect it to happen – or rather I knew it might happen, but I had hoped that I would never have to set eyes on Billy Bulldog ever again. I felt immensely degraded. I had been used right to the very end. I couldn't wait to get away from Highbroom and Crowborough: I was feeling scared and angry and there were still two days before I could be sure of a safe haven away from Billy Bulldog.

The petty spite of the staff also continued right to the end. Throughout my years at Highbroom the staff, mainly Mr Jenton, had confiscated items which belonged to me. There was a sleeping bag, a typewriter and the trilby hat. There were probably countless others I'd forgotten about. When I came to leave Highbroom at last I presumed that my property would be given back. I had asked Mr Jenton about my things and he had said I could have them back when I left. But Mr Jenton kept my confiscated belongings or, to put it another way, Mr Jenton stole my hat, my sleeping bag and my typewriter. All those years Mr Jenton had punished me for 'stealing' and now he had stolen from me. I later managed to claim from Barnardo's to replace the items Mr Jenton had stolen from me.

I left Beacon School on 22 May 1980. On Saturday 23 May I was in Mr Jenton's car heading towards Kingston-upon-Thames. Although I had no real chance to say goodbye to my friends, I didn't feel in any way upset about leaving Crowborough. I was not told my exact release date, so when it finally happened it came so quickly that it was more of a shock than anything else.

We set off quite early on that Saturday morning. Throughout the journey I didn't speak a word. As we travelled through familiar countryside I felt at ease. I was at last getting out of Highbroom, out of Crowborough. The sun was shining brightly and I thought to myself, I have waited a very long time for this day, and I intend to remember every moment of it. Yesterday I left school, today I am leaving Highbroom and Crowborough. It was a lot to take in all at once. I had difficulty in holding back my emotions for I wanted to shout out, 'I've done it, I've done it, I've done it! I'm free!' The feeling of relief and happiness that my sentence at Crowborough was over made me feel I would burst open with the pressure of emotions.

As the signs started to give directions to Kingston, my euphoria began to subside a little. I started to wonder what was going to happen in the future. Although I couldn't really begin to imagine what life had in store for me in Kingston, I felt sure it couldn't be anything like Crowborough.

But my sense of freedom was short-lived. As the car entered the drive of the hostel in Kingston, I realised my true freedom had not yet arrived.

# Postscript: Who Cares?

Immediately after I arrived at the Kingston hostel I was forced to look for work. The hostel work ethic meant that every resident had to have a job or they were outcasts. Within a couple of weeks I found employment in a restaurant in Kingston. I hated the job and left after three months. Then I got work as a trainee butcher, another job I hated. My employer sacked me after three months as I was useless at it. Luckily I had another job to go to in a fruit shop, where I stayed for about three months before I got the sack. My employers thought I was stealing from the till, which I most definitely refute. After a couple of weeks being unemployed I managed to get a job in a factory in Kingston. I didn't hate it, but it really wasn't what I wanted to do.

During my first year at the hostel I was assaulted by the man in charge and left with a black eye. I also had a few confrontations with members of staff. Just before the end of my first year there, I absconded along with three other residents. I was on the run for a whole month, a glorious achievement.

My reluctant return meant that I had to play the system with the promise of parole on the condition of good behaviour. I still hated being in care and believed that I had done my stint. Weren't seventeen years enough? Not long after my little escapade I got a job in a warehouse. I liked the people I worked with and didn't mind the work, and I stayed there for just over two years.

At nineteen I was still in care and nothing much in my life

seemed to be going right. One bright spot was that, when I had saved some money, I was able to go on my first foreign holiday, to Spain. Yet, as so often in my childhood, a brief, glorious break from my unhappy existence and the glimpse of another life served only to heighten my despair when I returned. When I got back from Spain, I went into deep depression. I began to hate my dead-end job, I hated the fact that I was still in care and, in addition, I was very upset that a holiday romance was over. My future looked irretrievably bleak. My depression grew steadily worse and on 12 September 1983 I tried to kill myself by taking an overdose of thirty-three paracetamols. I was taken to Kingston Hospital, where I refused to have my stomach pumped. I desperately wanted to die, and besides, I had heard from other people that a stomach pump was a horrible and painful experience. After some arguments with doctors, nurses and a member of the hostel staff, the hospital brought in a psychiatrist, which only angered me. I went beserk. I was hyperactive and shouting at everyone. The hospital staff, seeing that the 'shrink' tactic didn't work, then threatened to section me under the Mental Health Act. I knew that to be serious shit so I reluctantly agreed to take some more tablets and medicine which would counteract the pills I had taken. I left hospital the next day feeling even more depressed than ever. Not only was I still alive, but I had now acquired a new pejorative label: 'mental'. The hospital staff suggested that I should go to outpatients to see the psychiatrist. Needless to say I ignored that advice. I was extremely wary of shrinks.

Back at the hostel, the staff were desperately trying to play down my attempted suicide, claiming that I hadn't really taken the tablets and that anyway, since I was nineteen I was not officially in their care. Rather than face the truth that I was very ill and had tried to kill myself the staff took an ambivalent attitude. Consequently I was left to deal with my depression alone. Being so ill I was unable to work and had to resign from my warehouse job.

I then spent some time unemployed before working as a temp at various agencies in Kingston, still very depressed but trying to get by as best I could. In early December 1983 I sent a letter and Christmas card to my Aunt Dorothy. She promptly replied with a letter and a card. In the letter she informed me that my father had died of a heart attack and had been buried in November. I didn't know what to do or how to feel. I couldn't mourn my father for I had never known him, but I felt sorrow knowing that I would never get to know him now.

That evening, after receiving the letter, I went and spoke to the staff. Then I rang Aunt Dorothy. We chatted for a while and I arranged to go over and see her. A member of staff drove me over to Kent. We both went in and my auntie made tea. I hadn't seen her since I was fourteen, but she hadn't changed one little bit. After a very emotional conversation we left, but I made and kept a promise to keep in regular contact with her.

By January 1984 the hostel staff were hounding me to get a permanent job. They didn't approve of temporary work because I didn't always work a full week. I was sure this incessant nagging had nothing to do with my working hours or pay but was harassment for the sake of it, and it wore me down. I took a permanent job as a kitchen porter. I loathed both the job and the working environment and did it purely to keep the hostel people off my back. However, I decided not to tell them about it just to see how long it would take them to notice. Sure enough, the badgering continued. One evening a member of staff kept on and on about it until I could stand it no longer. I informed him that while he and other members of staff had been having a go at me for weeks and weeks I had had a job all the time. I explained to him that it just went to show they didn't know what they were talking about.

My sixth permanent full-time job was not to last – I couldn't face it day in, day out. After about seven weeks I started messing around and taking days off, and eventually walked out. Luckily, however, an employment agency found me another post within a couple of weeks, working in the reprographic department of the head office of a large company.

Although my job was only photocopying, to me it was, to begin with at least, really good, offering by far the best working conditions and hours I had encountered since leaving school.

At the end of May 1984 I left Kingston hostel, and left care. A friend of mine from the hostel and I moved to a flat in Surbiton. I could hardly believe it when it happened. I was now free. My twentieth birthday was less than three weeks away but I kidded myself that at least I had got out as a teenager.

September 1964 to May 1984.

Twenty years in care for a crime I didn't commit.